CINEMA SOUTHWEST

CINEMA SOUTHWEST

AN ILLUSTRATED GUIDE TO
THE MOVIES AND THEIR LOCATIONS

JOHN A. MURRAY

CANYONLANDS
NATURAL HISTORY ASSOCIATION

for Christine

The text type was set in Stone Print
The display type was set in ITC Blair Bold
Composed in the United States of America
Art direction by David Jenney
Designed by Jennifer Schaber
Edited by Stephanie Bucholz and Brad Melton
Production supervised by Lisa Brownfield
Film stills research by Jeb Stuart Rosebrook

Printed in China by Midas Printing Company Limited

www.cnha.org

First Printing, March 2000

First CNHA Printing, December 2008

12   11   10   09   08   1   2   3   4   5

ISBN 13: 978-0937407141

Murray, John A., 1954–
    Cinema southwest : an illustrated guide to the movies and
their locations / John A. Murray.
        p.   cm.
    Includes bibliographical references and index.
    ISBN 0-87358-747-2 (alk. paper)
    1. Motion picture locations—Southwestern States—
Guidebooks. 2. Western films—United States—History and
criticism. I. Title.

PN1995.67.S645 M87 2000
384'.8'02579–dc21   99-055282

4M/12-08

COVER: *John Ford filming a scene for* THE SEARCHERS *(Warner Bros., 1956) in Monument Valley. Courtesy Bud and Louise DeWald Collection.*

BACK COVER: *John Wayne, John Ford, and Cornelius Vanderbilt Whitney examine film on the set of* THE SEARCHERS. *Whitney helped produce and finance the film. Courtesy Bud and Louise DeWald Collection.*

FRONTIS: *A rare, behind-the-scenes look at* THE SEARCHERS *shows John Ford directing John Wayne as Ethan Edwards and Jeffrey Hunter as Martin Pawley. Courtesy Bud and Louise DeWald Collection.*

OPPOSITE: *Arguably the King of Western Film, John Ford's empty chair sits like a throne to the late director. Courtesy Bud and Louise DeWald Collection.*

PAGE VI-VII: *Arizona's Monument Valley has inspired filmmakers for decades. Courtesy John Murray.*

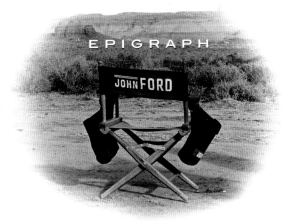

"That [Monument Valley], an ancient sea floor with sandstone massifs jutting out of a red and featureless plain, the cliffs worn into soaring pinnacles by centuries of weathering, was chosen by Ford as the setting for his most famous films confirms the conviction that its landscape is central to Ford's view of the world . . . it is an area with little relation to the conventional geography of the West, a patchwork of natural features lending itself to subjective interpretation. To Ford, Monument Valley was appealing precisely because its features were sufficiently unusual to be free of conventional emotional associations; its plains and pinnacles did not share a generally agreed symbolic meaning as does a mountain range or a field of wheat, and they could therefore be used as Ford used more easily manipulated natural phenomena like wind or light, as symbols of a particular morality, a view of the world that would be reflected in the world itself. Ford's style is perfectly mirrored in this landscape, the measured flow of his theme in the flat plain, its dramatic peaks in the sudden eruptions of stone around which he always sets his major battles and dramatic confrontations, while his concept of society, in which man, orderly and respectful of rules, maintains the natural order in the shadow of unassailable principles, seems emblematised in his films of the cavalry fighting and dying among the valley's stones while overhead the omnipresent clouds suggest a higher reality of mind and of spirit to which we are all subservient."

—John Baxter in *The Cinema of John Ford* (1971)

CONTENTS

PREFACE

Someday this country will be a good place where boys like you can grow up safe.

—HENRY FONDA, as Marshall Wyatt Earp, in
John Ford's *My Darling Clementine* (1946)

It is impossible to travel any distance in the Southwest without encountering a landscape that has appeared in an American film. Everywhere—deserts, mountains, canyons, prairies, rivers, forests, sea coasts—are scenes that have been memorialized on screen. Indeed, the Southwest at times seems more a country of the mind, a province of the human imagination, a theatrical construct of Panavision cameras and Hollywood editing studios, than a geographic region of North America. Within an hour's drive from Moab, Utah, for example, one can stand on the same overlook from which Jesus Christ delivered the Sermon on the Mount in *The Greatest Story Ever Told,* or follow the same dusty canyon trail used by Indiana Jones in *Indiana Jones and the Last Crusade,* or, on a less grand scale, climb the same slickrock that Billy Crystal scrambled up in *City Slickers.* Further south, in Monument Valley, the buttes and mesas are synonymous with the film legacy of John Wayne. In California and Nevada, the deserts and mountains evoke the films of such venerable actors as Humphrey Bogart, Marilyn Monroe, and Clint Eastwood. New Mexico calls to mind, among others, the vision quest of Jack Nicholson, Dennis Hopper, and Peter Fonda in *Easy Rider.* Texas will forever be known as McMurtry Country.

How exactly are we to define the Southwest? Is it somehow restricted solely to those areas where cactus and coral snakes, roadrunners and rock hounds are found? Or is it something larger and more comprehensive, a sprawling region of light and sky and limited rain? For the purposes of this book, the Southwest will be defined, both cartographically and culturally, in terms of what it lacks: water. It can be broadly delineated as a region of scarce precipitation. By these terms, the Southwest ranges from the arid sagebrush parks of the southern Rockies to the sun-baked sand dunes of Death Valley, from the short-grass prairie of the old Santa Fe Trail to the saguaro-studded deserts of the Mexican borderlands. It includes the palm-lined streets of Los Angeles and the neon-lit strips of Las Vegas and Reno, as well as the dry Pacific coast from San Diego to Big Sur. It takes in parts of Oklahoma and extreme southwestern Kansas, much of Texas, all of southern Colorado and southern Utah, vast portions of California south of Mono Lake and Nevada south of Reno, and the entire states of Arizona and New Mexico. It does not include desert locations in Mexico, Italy, Spain, Portugal, Morocco, or Australia, all of which have been represented (quite brilliantly at times) in films as being the American Southwest.

OPPOSITE: *Peter Fonda as Captain America in Dennis Hopper's* EASY RIDER *(Columbia, 1969). Courtesy Photofest.*

This is a book about the timeless landscapes of the Southwest, about places that are as lovely and special and historic as any on earth. It is a book about the ability of films to stir the heart to laughter or to tears, to speak the truth about injustice, and to celebrate the beauty of nature wild and human. It is a book about the power of films to change the world, if only one darkened theater at a time. It is a book about the enduring gift that is fine art. It is a book, above all, that is meant to be

Bruce Beresford's TENDER MERCIES *(Universal, 1983) is the poignant story of second chances when an alcoholic, ex-singer, Robert Duvall (Mac Sledge), starts a new life with a widow, Tess Harper (Rosa Lee Wadsworth), and her young son, Allan Hubbard (Sonny). Courtesy Eddie Brandt's Saturday Matinee.*

used, to be kept out and read, and to be taken along as a trip planner when the urge finally comes (it will) to see these locations. The more people know about these locations, some of which are imperiled (as with Professor Valley in Utah), all of which are essential parts of our cultural heritage, the more people will be there to support and ultimately preserve them.

Any work covering such a vast area and extensive subject must be by its very nature selective. In Texas alone—a minor state for filmmaking compared to California—over eight hundred films have been made. Inevitably, many decisions were made about what films to include and, just as difficult, which films not to include. Films were selected roughly based on three criteria: significant use of the Southwestern landscape (as in *Stagecoach* and its representations of the Monument Valley environment), aesthetic achievement (as in the truth-telling of *Lonely Are the Brave, The Misfits,* and *Tender Mercies*), and/or cinematic importance (a film like *Hang 'Em High,* for example, may not technically be a classic film, but the Southwestern landscape was used significantly and the picture had a surprising impact, in terms of stimulating a broader discussion in the popular culture).

I have many thanks. First, and most fully, much appreciation to my former editor Erin Murphy and Northland's marketing director Karen Anderson, for coming up with the idea for this book. Thanks also to Stephanie Bucholz and Brad Melton, my editors at Northland. *Cinema Southwest* could not have come into being without the assistance of national park personnel in the Southwestern region, officials at a number of city and state film commissions, and the staff at the Academy of Motion Picture's Margaret Herrick Library in Beverly Hills, California. The book is in many ways a collaborative project involving all of these entities. I would like to thank the state film commissions of Arizona, California (Suzanne Archuleta), Colorado (Stephanie Two Eagles), New Mexico (Linda Hutchinson and Kelly Cosandaey), Nevada, and Texas; as well as the city film commissions of Phoenix, Arizona; Los Angeles, California; Lone Pine, California; Page, Arizona; Sedona, Arizona; Yuma, Arizona; Prescott, Arizona; and Moab, Utah (Kari Murphy).

Clark Gable as Gay Langland and Montgomery Clift as Perce Howland in John Huston's essay on human loneliness, THE MISFITS *(UA, 1961). Courtesy of the Academy of Motion Picture Arts and Sciences.*

I would especially like to thank Faye Thompson at the Academy of Motion Pictures, and Kate McGrade, for their warm hospitality during my visit to Los Angeles. Eileen Martinez at Glen Canyon National Recreation Area, Blaire Davenport at Death Valley National Park, Maureen Ogeltree at Grand Canyon National Park, Alice Allen at Santa Monica National Recreation Area, and Carol Yeston at Arches National Park were all most helpful. A word of special appreciation goes to Claire Brandt of Eddie Brandt's Saturday Matinee; Louise DeWald; Allen C. Reed; Jeb J. Rosebrook; Jack Dykinga; Howard Mendelbaum and Jay Weissberg of Photofest; Mary Corliss and Terry Geesken of the Museum of Modern Art; John Nichols; Cristina Santos of Simon & Schuster; Bob Early and Connie Boch of *Arizona Highways;* and the staff at the Academy of Motion Picture Arts and Sciences, all of whom were instrumental in providing film still photos, lobby cards, and other images.

One of the more enjoyable aspects of this project was the four-week, five-thousand-mile research trip through the Southwest I made in October and November of 1998. It was among the most enlightening experiences of my life. At forty-four I had the opportunity to experience the sort of slow, solitary, and thorough journey across a far country on a singular mission that most people can only undertake upon retirement. I'll never forget camping on the banks of the Colorado River near Moab, the breeze rustling through the yellow leaves of the cottonwood trees, the river murmuring quietly below; or the three days of rain and fog at my campsite in Monument Valley, the sudden break in the clouds and the Dantean light illuminating the inner valley; or my camp in the Alabama Hills at the base of Mount Whitney, and rising before dawn to watch Orion set into the Sierras as the eastern rim of the world turned red. These are the moments that make book-writing not just a vocation but an alternate way of being.

Finally I would like to thank my son, for whom everything I do is related, and my father, whose friendship is a daily reminder of what is important in life.

FABLES AND DISTANCES

Jack, I want to tell you something. The world that you and Paul live in doesn't exist. It isn't real.
> —GERRI BONDI (played by Gena Rowland) to Jack Burns (played by Kirk Douglas), in *Lonely Are the Brave* (1962)

I am sitting on a rock overlooking Monument Valley. It is the hour before sunrise. The sky to the west, over Oljeto Mesa, is still sprinkled with a few stars. The sky to the east, over the distant Chuska Mountains, is as pink as the palm of my hand. Even as I watch, a lens of red light is forming on the horizon. Before me are three great buttes—Left Mitten, Merrick, and Right Mitten. The names may not be familiar, but almost everyone has seen the formations, for they have been featured in dozens of films. All around the landscape is perfectly flat, and then suddenly there are these three heavy solid rocks, each rising to the height of a one-hundred-story building. If they were not magnificent enough, there are mesas and buttes and isolated spires made of the same sandstone scattered at wide spaces in every direction. To the north are Castle Butte, Brigham's Tomb, Big Indian, Bear and Rabbit, King-on-His-Throne, Setting Hen, and Eagle Mesa. To the south are Elephant Butte, Camel Butte, Clye Butte, Big Chair, and Spearhead Mesa.

As the light comes up on the earth, the country begins to reveal its secrets. It is a desert land, spare and disciplined, and there is no fat on it. The colors are dry and sun-washed, like the colors of Anasazi pottery sherds. The floor of the desert is covered with reddish-brown sand, dotted here and there with rabbitbrush and sage, prickly pear cactus, and barbed yucca. Along the winding stream courses, junipers and piñon grow, branched in delicate ways and colored olive-green, like bonsai. Otherwise there are no trees, only sand dunes and Martian rocks and plants with small waxy leaves and clustered thorns. The early-morning air is cool and fresh, and scented with the smell of sage. Sometimes there is a breeze that is as cold as ice water. Other times, there are warmer currents, as the air of earth and heaven begin to mix.

First light across such a landscape comes with a force unknown to dwellers of the city. The amber rays and beams move and shift powerfully across the land, striking first the mesa tops and then moving downward. The fractured walls of the buttes display stronger hues than the rest of the landscape, as if they have, over the ages, absorbed the fire of more than one Arizona sunrise. They seem to glow with an inner light. After a few minutes, as the valley becomes more fully illuminated, the beauty of the place rises to an entirely new level and you think, *this is the giant outdoor theater in which some of the finest movies in the*

OPPOSITE: *Monument Valley's giant volcanic plugs and sandstone monoliths have served as the backdrop for many Western films including* THE VANISHING AMERICAN *(Paramount, 1925),* 2001: A SPACE ODYSSEY *(Larry Spangler Productions, 1968), and* FORREST GUMP *(Paramount, 1993). Courtesy John Murray.*

American Southwest were filmed. Here, for example, on the dirt track below the rock on which I sit, the little wooden stage from Lordsburg, drawn by a team of six horses, made its perilous journey through the desert wilderness in *Stagecoach*. A decade later, in *She Wore a Yellow Ribbon*, John Wayne rode up the same route as Captain Nathan Brittles, searching for the Indians who had murdered the paymaster. A mile behind me, on the highway, Jack Nicholson, Dennis Hopper, and Peter Fonda roared by on their Harley Davidsons in *Easy Rider*. More recently, Tom Hanks jogged up the same pavement in *Forrest Gump*. Everything about Southwestern films that we experience—from the hushed moment in the neighborhood theater when the lights go down to the bright evening in March when the Oscars are awarded—begins in windy, sun-washed places like this, far from the crowded cities and close to the pure inspiration of landscape.

The sun begins to have some real warmth to it and soon I am joined by a Navajo dog, a small-boned pilgrim with a short, nondescript coat and a bushy tail filled with all manner of seeds, twigs, and pine cones. Shortly his brother joins him. They both appear, in the narrow shape of the skull and the grizzled muzzle and a certain wildness in the eyes, to have been fathered or perhaps grandfathered by a coyote. But they have friendly personalities, and I turn back and happily follow them toward the campground, where the world is stirring again. It will be a good day, for there are no bad days in such a place, up close to the blue Arizona sky and among some of the grandest scenery in the world.

If the Southwest has a heart—an aesthetic, historical, geographic center—it is here, in Monument Valley. The valley resides at the dusty core of the most lovely desert of all, the Painted. All Southwestern trails eventually lead to the valley and all standards of beauty—either wild or human—ultimately issue forth from the valley. We can imagine a Southwest without Bryce Canyon, or even without Zion, just as we can imagine a person without an arm or a leg, but a Southwest without Monument Valley is inconceivable. It is the beating heart, the central gallery, the involuted essence of a vast region, and its features reveal much about why so many wonderful films have been made in the Southwest.

In Monument Valley, and places like it across the Southwest, filmmakers have consistently found a landscape that both frames and elevates character. Such monumental features as the Mitten Buttes and Merrick Butte immediately lift action and character to heroic stature. Elsewhere, more empty desert landscapes serve strongly to focus viewer attention on dialogue, character, and action. Across the region, these unique landscapes quietly do some of the storytelling work of the screenwriter and the director, as setting becomes a metaphor—the harshness of existence, the ethical bleakness of modern life, the isolation of the individual—from which viewers can then form their own abstractions. In olden days storytellers had only the flat limestone stage at Epidaurus, Greece, or the cramped wooden stage at the Globe in England in which to create and populate a world. In our time, through the medium of film, our theaters stretch from the sand dunes at our feet to the purple mountains on the horizon, from the cumulus clouds floating overhead to the furthest visible stars.

I didn't know anything about the OK Corral at the time, but Harry Carey knew about it, and he had asked Wyatt [Earp] and Wyatt had described it fully. As a matter of fact, he had drawn it out on paper, a sketch of the entire thing. Wyatt had said, "I was not a good shot; I had to get close to a man." So in My Darling Clementine, *we did it exactly the way it had been. They didn't just walk up the street and start banging away at each other; it was a clever military maneuver.*

—JOHN FORD, in an interview with Peter Bogdanovich
[from his book *John Ford* (1978)]

OPPOSITE: *John Wayne as Captain Nathan Brittles is a career cavalryman on his last patrol in John Ford's* SHE WORE A YELLOW RIBBON *(RKO, 1949). Courtesy Museum of Modern Art.*

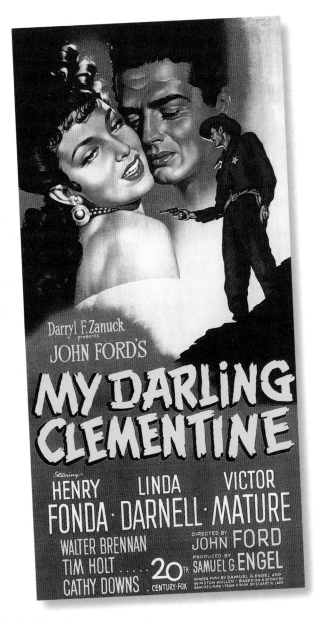

Henry Fonda (Wyatt Earp), Linda Darnell (Chihuahua), and Victor Mature (Doc Holliday) tell the story of the shoot-out at the OK Corral in John Ford's MY DARLING CLEMENTINE *(20th-Fox, 1946). Courtesy Eddie Brandt's Saturday Matinee.*

The origins of film, unlike the origins of other art forms (such as drama) are well known. The story begins in 1861, about twenty-five years after the invention of the daguerreotype, or chemically based photograph, when a man named Coleman Sellers in Philadelphia arranged a series of upright consecutive photographs on a circular table. When the table was spun, the visual impression was created, in the rapidly spinning blur of images, of sequential movement. As children we applied the same principle when, bored in the back of the classroom, we opened a tablet of paper and drew a figure running in different positions on twenty or so consecutive pages. When the pages were turned quickly our eyes perceived movement—often, a cartoon caricature of the teacher running from one point to another with exaggerated movements.

Mr. Sellers, a machinist by trade, christened his mechanical creation the "Kinematoscope." A few years later, another industrious Philadelphian (Ben Franklin would have been proud) invented the "Phasmotrope," in which a rapid series of photographs again produced the perception of fluid motion. The next step—phase three in the narrative—was the most important. It occurred in 1877 when Eadweard Muybridge, an English-born American photographer, won a $25,000 bet (a small fortune in 1877) by proving that a galloping horse does in fact periodically lift all four hooves from the ground at the same time. Muybridge accomplished this feat—which forever changed the way artists painted horses—by arranging twenty-four cameras in a row and attaching the twenty-four shutter releases to consecutive trip wires. As the horse galloped by, his or her legs pulled and broke the wires in sequence, producing twenty-four separate images, one of which conclusively settled the ancient debate.

The final essential ingredient was supplied by the genius of Thomas Edison, also known as "The Wizard of Menlo Park." Ten years after the Muybridge experiment, Edison (who slept four hours a night and tinkered in his shop for the other twenty) devised a primitive apparatus that would record visual motion simultaneously with the Edison phonograph, which recorded sound. In 1893 the U.S. government granted patents to Edison for the world's first motion picture camera, called the Kinetograph, and the world's first motion picture viewer, called the Kinetoscope. One year later a Kinetoscope parlor—the world's first movie theater—opened in New York City. For a quarter (about ten dollars in today's currency) a customer could watch such epic masterpieces as *Horseshoeing* and *Barber Shop*. Despite the mundane offerings, the humble theater was an instant success, and almost overnight Kinetoscope parlors were found in San Francisco, London, and Paris.

Gradually over the next few years motion pictures were incorporated into the traveling vaudeville programs (vaudeville consisted of singing, dancing, and informal skits) that were then popular in both big city and small town venues. These early films involved short spans of film and were restricted to a single staged scene shot from a heavy wooden camera mounted on a fixed tripod. Some of the silents were comedic and others were dramatic (human nature being what it is, others were neither comedic nor dramatic). By far, the most influential of these early pioneering films was Edwin S. Porter's *The Great Train Robbery*, which was made in 1903. Porter's film, which ran an unprecedented twelve minutes, is generally considered to be the first narrative story told on film, with an effective beginning, middle, and end. The movie was a surprising box-office success, and opened the bulging wallets of cautious investors poised to provide capital for the largely untested film industry. Within two years, there were literally hundreds of Nickelodeon theaters (so named because they cost five cents) scattered across the country. The horses were out of the gate, and the race that would thunder through the twentieth century was on—the race to make money from this new art form.

It is not insignificant, in terms of this book, that the first unified movie was a Western (albeit a Western filmed in the wilds of New Jersey). Since the beginning of film the dominant genre in the Southwest has been the Western. In truth, the Western as a form of narrative began long before film. The sources are as diverse as the lineaments of the frontier: the historical recreations of Buffalo Bill's traveling Wild West Shows, the dramatic paintings of Frederic Remington and others, and the popular writings of such national figures as George Armstrong Custer, Mark Twain, Theodore Roosevelt, Bret Harte, and Owen Wister. The central themes of the Western—courage under fire *(Fort Apache)*, good versus evil *(High Plains Drifter)*, the corrupting influence of power *(Salt of the Earth)*, the individual versus society *(The Milagro Beanfield War)*, the wrath of nature *(The Grapes of Wrath)*, the importance of love *(The Misfits)*, the centrality of the family *(East of Eden)*, the resilience of the spirit *(Jeremiah Johnson)*—have remained constant over more than a century.

Although New York was at first the capital of the filming world, William Selig, Edison's chief competitor, moved his studio, the Selig Polyscope Company, to Hollywood in 1909. Within a short time Los Angeles became the base of operations for the film industry. The reasons were obvious—more sunny days (for outdoor shooting) and more diverse landscapes than back East. Even in the early years of film, the studios often took their productions into the countryside so that scenes could be shot in realistic settings and under natural light. This added to the verisimilitude of the film and also decreased the amount of money the studios had to invest (no expensive indoor or outdoor sets to construct, no electrical bills for indoor lighting, no urban noise or distractions). Initially, the studios used old cattle ranches in the Santa Monica Mountains north of Los Angeles. Actors such as G. M. Anderson ("Bronco Billy") performed at these locations in Westerns such as *The Bandit Makes Good*. Soon, the studios began to wander farther afield.

As early as 1915 Selig Films was producing one-reel Westerns featuring Tom Mix in Las Vegas, New Mexico. In 1920 films began to be shot on location in the Alabama Hills near Lone Pine, California. Two years later the first Tom Mix film was filmed in the Alabama Hills, and not long after that an adaptation of Zane Grey's novel *Riders of the Purple Sage* was filmed at the same location. John Ford produced his four-hour epic *The Iron Horse* on location near Reno, Nevada, in 1924, and a year later George Seitz made *The Vanishing American* in

Nasja as "The Owl" was one of 10,000 Navajos who were in George Seitz's THE VANISHING AMERICAN *(Paramount, 1925), which was adapted from Zane Grey's novel of the same name. Courtesy Eddie Brandt's Saturday Matinee.*

Monument Valley, Arizona. Other popular filming locations discovered and developed during this early period include Old Pariah, a scenic ghost town west of Page, Arizona; the redrock and sand dune landscapes around Kanab, Utah; the high timbered mountains near Canon City, Colorado; the cactus country surrounding Tucson, Arizona; and Death Valley (where the silent classic *Greed* was filmed). All of these

locations were ideal for the Western, which was from the beginning one of the most popular, and therefore dominant, film genres.

Several key developments, in terms of film technology and of the film industry, occurred in the first few decades of the twentieth century. The first was the creation and refinement of color film, which would become increasingly important after the 1930s (beginning with *Gone With the Wind*, filmed in Technicolor, 1939). The second was the invention of simultaneous sound-recording technology, which led to major motion pictures with sound as early as 1929 (most notably, the Oscar-winning film *In Old Arizona* with Warner Baxter in 1929 and *The Virginian* with Gary Cooper in 1929). The third was the emergence of the five major film companies, Paramount, Fox, MGM, Warner Brothers, and RKO, and three secondary film companies, Universal, Columbia, and United Artists, as the chief entities of the film world.

The advantage of the big studios was that they offered creative artists—screenwriters, directors, actors, technical managers—a stable environment in which to make movies regularly. The studios oversaw everything—screenwriting, casting, filming, editing, production, marketing, and distribution—with legendary efficiency. The disadvantage was that the studios, being profit-driven enterprises, tended to stifle the creativity of their talent and rely on formulaic approaches, particularly with respect to Westerns (a problem, industry- and genre-wide, even today). A film was considered a product, an actor was regarded as a business expense, and the studios were run much like automobile factories. Their purpose was not aesthetic, but was rather to maximize profit. This systemic problem first became evident in 1919 when a number of actors—Charlie Chaplin, Douglas Fairbanks, and William S. Hart—issued a "declaration of independence" against the corporate film establishment and formed their own company. The old studio system of the silent film era was recently parodied in the film *Three Amigos!*, with comedians Chevy Chase, Steve Martin, and Martin Short playing three out-of-work actors (filmed primarily at the Old Tucson film set).

Despite the inherent flaws of the corporate system, some excellent Southwestern movies were made as early as the 1930s, and this occurred

Martin Short (Ned Nederlander), Chevy Chase (Dusty Bottoms), and Steve Martin (Lucky Day) are unemployed actors who travel to a Mexican village to play the roles of bandit fighters and are unaware that it is the real thing in John Landis' THREE AMIGOS! *(Orion, 1986). Courtesy Eddie Brandt's Saturday Matinee.*

even with the substantial economic effects of the 1929 stock market crash and the Great Depression on the film companies and their audiences. In a decade that saw such pedestrian creations as the movies of Zorro, Rin-Tin-Tin, Buck Jones, Hoot Gibson, and the singing cowboys (Gene Autry and Roy Rogers), the studios also managed to produce such films as *Gunga Din*, *The Lives of the Bengal Lancers*, and *The Charge of the Light Brigade* (all filmed in the Alabama Hills near Lone Pine, California). One of the decade's most interesting Southwestern films was *The Petrified Forest* (shot in 1936 on a Hollywood set that portrayed the Arizona desert, as well as on location in Petrified Forest National Park). The production gave the world its first good look at three extraordinary actors: Humphrey Bogart, Bette Davis, and Leslie Howard (who later portrayed Ashley Wilkes in *Gone With the Wind*).

By far, the finest Southwestern film of the decade (some might say, of all time) was John Ford's *Stagecoach* (1939). The film was based on the Ernest Haycox short story "Stage to Lordsburg," which, in turn, was an adaptation of Guy de Maupassant's well-known tale "Ball of Fat" (the French sounds better—"Boule de suif"). *Stagecoach* relates the experiences of a group of ordinary people on a dangerous journey through a desert wilderness. Ford's choice of a filming location— Monument Valley—for this major studio production would change American cinema, and the national vision of the Southwest, forever (as would his choice of a lead actor in John Wayne).

Three events shaped the 1940s and the 1950s: the Second World War (which brought new technology into the film world), the explosive development of television (which constituted the first serious challenge to film), and the Cold War (which led to an unprecedented pessimism and darkness in all the arts). This mid-century period can be seen in two ways—as both the culmination of fifty years of filmmaking and as a transitional phase when new approaches and new themes were beginning to transform the industry. Although films on traditional themes continued to be made—*High Sierra* (the outlaw movie), *My Darling Clementine* (the historical movie), and *High Noon* (the gunfighter movie)—filmmakers also demonstrated an increasing willingness to explore new territory. This included themes of social injustice *(Sergeant Rutledge, Bad Day at Black Rock)* and economic injustice *(The Grapes of Wrath, The Salt of the Earth)*. If there is one movie that best expresses the conflict of the period, it is John Ford's *The Searchers*, which was filmed, as with nine of Ford's other Westerns, in Monument Valley. John Wayne portrayed Ethan Edwards, an elusive, dark character with as many vices as virtues.

One of the most important developments of the period occurred in the 1950s when the studio system—which had held actors under exclusive contract to one company—began to break down. Much of this change occurred because of the efforts of the "Rat Pack," an infor-

Andy Devine (Buck), John Wayne (the Ringo Kid), and Claire Trevor (Dallas) are part of a group of nine people from different backgrounds who face danger and uncertainty on a bumpy road to Lordsburg, New Mexico, in John Ford's STAGECOACH *(UA, 1939). Courtesy Eddie Brandt's Saturday Matinee.*

mal group of influential actors first organized by Humphrey Bogart (and later led by Frank Sinatra). The 1950s also saw the emergence of several gifted new actors, including James Dean (who had a brief but brilliant career, with a riveting performance in the California-based *East of Eden*), Marilyn Monroe (whose 1956 movie *Bus Stop* was filmed partially in Arizona and California), and Clint Eastwood, who began appearing in the weekly television show *Rawhide* in 1958. It was also during this period that the prominent western actor Ronald Reagan [*Santa Fe Trail* (1940), *Law and Order* (1953), the television show *Death Valley Days* (1952–1975)], began to move from film into politics. Reagan had served as president of the Screen Actors Guild from 1947 through 1952, during the controversial period of anti-communist purges in the film industry. Reagan's abandonment of film, which resulted largely from his inability to obtain quality acting roles in the 1950s, would have considerable national and international import in the decades to come.

The 1960s began with a historical retrospective film—John Wayne's blockbuster, *The Alamo* (filmed in Bracketville, Texas)—that recalled the failed Western epics of Cecil B. DeMille from the 1930s (*Union Pacific, The Plainsman*). Soon it became evident that other, younger forces in Hollywood were prepared to move in entirely new directions. Three films stand out in this transitional period—*Lonely Are the Brave, Hud*, and *The Misfits*. Each painted an unflinchingly realistic portrait of life in the modern Southwest. As the sixties matured, the changes in filmmaking became even more bold, as evidenced in such movies as *Bonnie and Clyde* (a heightened level of screen violence), *Butch Cassidy and the Sundance Kid* (the professional outlaw as popular anti-hero), and *Easy Rider* (one of the most original stories ever told on film). The seventies continued along this path of free-spirited innovation in such films as *The Last Picture Show, High Plains Drifter,* and *The Electric Horseman*. The decade ended with a lifetime achievement Oscar for John Wayne.

Just as the 1950s are known as the decade when television revolutionized visual entertainment, the 1980s are known as the decade that

Don Murray as Beau Decker is a young cowboy who falls for a beautiful singer, Marilyn Monroe as Cherie, in Joshua Logan's BUS STOP *(20th-Fox, 1956). Courtesy Eddie Brandt's Saturday Matinee.*

saw the growth of videotape as a viable alternative to reel film. The effects of this new technology on the film industry have been massive. For one thing, audiences no longer find it necessary to go to movie theaters to view films. Any film, old or new, can be rented from a video store and watched at any time in the comfort of the home. Every living room has become a private screening theater. For another, the public has been able to increase their film literacy substantially and, not surprisingly, have developed a growing appreciation for the film classics (much as probably occurred when the first public book-lending libraries were created). Finally, the film companies have seen their profits steadily rise through secondary video sales, both in the United States and abroad. All of these changes have proven to be positive for the film industry and for the film arts.

During the 1980s and 1990s the landscapes of the Southwest continued to exert a powerful influence on filmmaking. One of the finest regional films of the period, *Tender Mercies,* featured the Oscar-winning performance of Robert Duvall as a down-on-his-luck country-western singer in rural Texas. Duvall went on to portray the Texas Ranger Augustus McCrae in *Lonesome Dove,* one of the most popular television productions ever made. The highlands of New Mexico—first featured in the silent films of Tom Mix—formed the majestic backdrop for Robert Redford's *The Milagro Beanfield War,* a film that addressed some of the social themes found in earlier Southwestern films such as *The Grapes of Wrath* and *The Salt of the Earth.* More recently, diverse motion pictures such as *Indiana Jones and the Last Crusade, Thelma and Louise, Rain Man, Forrest Gump,* and *Contact* have prominently featured Southwestern landscapes. In 1995 Nicholas Cage received an Oscar for his performance in *Leaving Las Vegas* and in 1997 Sharon Stone received an Oscar for her performance in *Casino.* Both films covered the same psychological terrain—alienated souls adrift in a Southwestern gambling town—explored nearly forty years earlier in *The Misfits.*

Over the past century Southwestern film has traveled a far distance. Once an experimental diversion seen by passersby in storefront arcades, Southwestern film is today one of the world's great art forms, capable of exploring with maturity and craft a full range of dramatic, historic, and epic stories and characters. Through these films audiences can vicariously live the life of the hero, or the outlaw; experience a catharsis of grief, or of love; or lose themselves in the grandeur of a vast landscape. In the years to come, Southwestern film is likely to become increasingly important in this respect, as people yearn more and more both for the myths and legends of the past and for a theatrical compass to guide them through the journey of life.

You boys don't look like you're from this part of the country.
—GEORGE HANSON (played by Jack Nicholson),
in *Easy Rider* (1969)

All narratives, all films, are ultimately grounded in nature, for nature consists of an endless series of stories. We have, for example the continual pageant of the seasons; the epic migrations of birds and beasts; the slow, steady passage of the days; the times of breeding and the times of birth; the building of great storms; the waxing and waning of the moon; the coming and going of comets and meteor showers; the life and death of stars and galaxies; the life and death of the universe itself. Each of these would be stories even if there were no people around to tell them as stories. They exist, have existed, and will always exist, separate from the human experience. They are part of the elemental narrative structure of the universe, which in turn is based on linear time and causality. Creating a film—creating any narrative—is an act very much at one with the natural processes of the world.

All films, then, begin with a story. The direct sources of the narrative vary considerably. Sometimes, the inspiration for a film is a short story, as when John Ford used James Bellah's story "Massacre" for his 1947 film *Fort Apache.* The challenge that filmmakers face with short fiction (including novellas), is that, because of its abbreviated length, short fiction focuses primarily on one action or character. Neither is ordinarily sufficient to sustain a full-length movie. More commonly, the source of a film is a novel, as when Willa Cather's novel *Cheyenne Autumn* inspired the 1964 John Ford film of the same title, or when Vardis Fisher's novel *Mountain Man* stirred Robert Redford to produce

OPPOSITE: *Robert Redford as the Sundance Kid and Paul Newman as Butch Cassidy are the leaders of the Hole-in-the-Wall Gang and leap off a cliff to escape a professional posse in George Hill's* BUTCH CASSIDY AND THE SUNDANCE KID *(20th-Fox, 1969). Courtesy Photofest.*

his 1972 film *Jeremiah Johnson*. Novels have multiple characters, explore at least two characters in depth, and include a substantial series of organically linked scenes. More often than not, they also have a parallel or contrapuntal subplot. Occasionally a play serves as the source of a film, as when William Inge's Pulitzer-prize winning drama *Picnic* was transformed into the 1955 Oscar-winning movie of the same name with William Holden and Kim Novak. Plays, with their close attention to character, revelatory action, and dialogue, can serve quite naturally as the basis for films.

Most of the time, though, a film is based upon an original screenplay—a dramatic script that is written by professional screenwriters, often in cooperation with industry executives, specifically for the purpose of creating a particular movie. This has been true since the earliest days of silent film and was demonstrably the case during the "Golden Age of Film," when such writers as William Faulkner and F. Scott Fitzgerald were regularly called in to write or rewrite screenplays. This practice has continued into more recent times, as when Arthur Miller wrote the screenplay for John Huston's 1961 film *The Misfits* or Dalton Trumbo was hired to transform Edward Abbey's novel *The Brave Cowboy* into the 1962 film *Lonely Are the Brave*. Screenplays (regardless of source) consist primarily of dialogue for characters, but may also contain detailed instructions regarding set location, camera placement, wardrobe, and even such matters as the sort of vocal tone, facial expression, and arm movements the actor should use. The screenplay provides the literal blueprint, or, to use another metaphor, the cellular DNA from which the film is made.

All successful movies, John Wayne once observed in a PBS interview toward the end of his career, are based on good characters. He might have gone further and observed that all successful narratives—whether around the water cooler, the wilderness campfire, or on the Broadway stage—are based on good characters. The key is what happens to the

Martin Ritt's HUD *(Paramount, 1963) is the story of conflicting values in a changing West and co-stars Paul Newman (Hud Bannon), Melvyn Douglas (Homer Bannon), and Brandon De Wilde (Lon Bannon). Courtesy of the Academy of Motion Picture Arts and Sciences.*

characters, and how they react to the internal conflicts or external complications that develop as the story progresses. Sometimes a film focuses on a dialectic—on the relationship between two major characters. This was the case in Sydney Pollack's 1979 film *The Electric Horseman*, which explored the relationship between the two opposing characters portrayed by Robert Redford and Jane Fonda. Other times, a film contains a buried triangle—three people whose interactions form the oldest structure in the geometry of drama. In *Hud*, for example, we have a triangle formed between the characters played by Melvyn Douglas (the traditional father), Paul Newman (the rebellious son), and Brandon de Wilde (the young nephew). Much of the work in creating a screenplay focuses on building strong characters, and then letting them interact naturally in ways the audience will find interesting or revealing.

OPPOSITE: *Carroll Baker as Deborah Wright is a young Quaker schoolteacher who is sympathetic to the Cheyenne during their long trek and feels responsible for her young charges in John Ford's* CHEYENNE AUTUMN *(Warner Bros., 1964). Courtesy Museum of Modern Art.*

Zabriske Point in Death Valley National Park. Courtesy John Murray.

Even in the 1930s, a major film production could cost as much as half a million dollars (as with John Ford's *Stagecoach*). John Wayne's 1960 film *The Alamo* cost nearly twelve million dollars to produce. In the 1990s a minimal budget for a major motion picture was in the neighborhood of $20 million. Sometimes (as with *The Alamo*) the creator of the film (in that case, Wayne himself) personally puts up the money for the film. This is a risky proposition but can pay dividends if the film is successful (as with Robert Duvall's 1998 film *The Apostle*).

Once on location, a film can be compared to a traveling circus. It enters a town—say Ridgeway, Colorado *(True Grit)* or Truchas, New Mexico *(The Milagro Beanfield War)*—and everything in that community is immediately changed. Whatever was news the day before is forgotten. From that point forward, the town citizenry will measure the life of their town in terms of "before the movie" and "after the movie." Most noticeably, a film brings a rich infusion of cash directly into the community—lodging, meals, gas, assorted daily supplies for, sometimes, hundreds of employees. Also, local people must be hired to assist the filmmakers in a myriad of ways—as drivers, carpenters, painters, plasterers, electricians, equipment handlers, laborers, technicians, wranglers, pilots, stunt doubles, set medics, cooks, production assistants, security guards, reclamation assistants, seamstresses, specialty experts (rock climbing, river rafting), and so forth. If shooting takes place on public land, then permits must be secured. Because films are such lucrative business, many towns (such as Moab, Utah, and Lone Pine, California) have for many decades had their own film commissions, which actively lobby the studios.

One day, after many weeks, the filmmakers disappear. They return to their studios, which are usually in southern California, and then begin the sometimes tortuous process of editing the raw footage into a complete film. Test audiences watch the early edited versions, and their reactions are carefully analyzed—Were the characters well portrayed?

After the screenplay has been more or less finalized, studio-backing and financing must be arranged. The latter is, increasingly, because of the labor and material costs involved, the most difficult part of the filmmaking process. Many a worthy project has languished for years, or ultimately died, in this delicate embryonic phase. Making films is an expensive business (compared to an artist painting a landscape or a writer composing a novel, both of which can be done at little expense).

OPPOSITE: *Filmed in rural New Jersey, Edwin S. Porter's* THE GREAT TRAIN ROBBERY *(Metro-Goldwyn, 1903) is considered by many to be the "first Western." Courtesy Eddie Brandt's Saturday Matinee.*

Did the dialogue seem real? Was the musical score satisfying? Was the ending too happy or too sad? Would they recommend the film to a friend? Somehow in all this process an enduring work of art is created (or not). A date for the release of the film is set (and occasionally postponed, as in James Cameron's *Titanic* or Stanley Kubrick's *Eyes Wide Shut*). The actors, and sometimes the director, travel to the major movie markets and make advance appearances. We see them on Jay Leno or David Letterman, talking about this or that aspect of filming. Articles are written. Critics weigh in, based on their previews. Suspense gathers. Finally the film is released (over three hundred films are released each year). If the film is bad, word spreads. If the film is good, word spreads. Once in a while, the film is wonderful, a classic, a story for the ages and made so by instantaneous popular acclaim, and everyone is happy (except perhaps a few of the younger actors, who are just learning about an ancient accounting practice in the film industry known as "keeping double books").

When the legend becomes fact, print the legend.
　　　　　　—Dutton Peabody (as played by Edmund O'Brien),
　　　　　　　　　　in *The Man Who Shot Liberty Valance* (1962)

Just as each person creates a personal history that is partly true and partly mythic, weaving fact and fiction—what happened and what sort of happened and what never happened—so do a nation's films provide their viewers with a series of narratives that soften the tragic, brighten the comic, and sharpen the historic. In the films of the Southwest—particularly those anchored in actual events (the battle at Apache Pass, the shoot-out at the OK Corral, the longhorn cattle drives)—we as a nation have fabricated an alternative and often illusory vision of ourselves and of the past. Part of this is rooted in the very function of art. When Shakespeare wrote that "our little lives are rounded with a sleep" he expressed a statement the wisdom of which is not often fully appreciated. Films, like dreams or fables, are part of the protective membrane that memory and imagination generate over

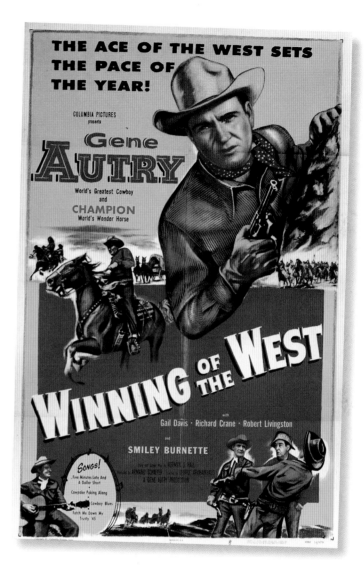

Gene Autry helps defend ranchers from outlaws in George Archainbaud's Winning of the West *(Columbia, 1953). Courtesy Eddie Brandt's Saturday Matinee.*

Opposite: The Lone Ranger *(1949–1957) television series was filmed in California's Alabama Hills. Courtesy John Murray.*

17

Gibson Gowland as John "Mac" McTeague and Jean Hersholt as Marcus Schouler in a scene from Erich von Stroheim's GREED *(Metro-Goldwyn, 1925). Courtesy Photofest.*

time, a metaphoric "sleep" that forms a boundary between each person, each society, and the cold hard surface of history.

A film is, to paraphrase Thoreau's familiar passage on books, at once more intimate and more universal than any other work of art. It combines the ancient art of storytelling with the modern art of photography, the visual effects of landscape and portrait painting with the dramatic power of theater, the notes and chords of music with the rhythm and force of poetry. It is the work of art nearest to life itself. It may be viewed by people in any land, speaking any language, at any time, and not only be watched but, with the addition of subtitles or overdubbing, understood and enjoyed. Movies are the treasured wealth of our time, and the highest creative expression of our age. They will be closely watched—for edification as well as entertainment—hundreds, thousands of years from now. Had Shakespeare been born in April of 1964 instead of April of 1564, he would now be active in films. He would be industriously writing and producing romances and comedies, histories and tragedies for the big screen, for film is to the Modern Age

what verse drama was to the Elizabethan Age. Film is the most versatile tool ever given to the human imagination to explore the heights and the depths, the travail and the splendor, the mysteries and the paradoxes of the human experience.

Look at the people emerging from a movie theater. Study their faces. Each has been changed, if only for the evening, by the experience. Their tired faces are brightened or saddened, flushed with laughter or reddened with tears, furrowed in thought or blank with amazement, by what they have just witnessed. They carry with them the still-fresh images and impressions from that other world—the eternal world of art. Their generation will grow old and die. All they know will change and be changed again, but the film they have just watched will remain, the characters as timeless as the carved figures on Keats' Grecian urn, the drama enduring like an island against the relentless flow of time. Films, these viewers can attest, have power. They can change the world, if only one darkened theater at a time. How many of us have dated a new era in our lives from the watching of a film?

Lonesome, eh? Yeah, I can see how you would get lonesome out here.
—MAD DOG EARLE (played by Humphrey Bogart),
in *High Sierra* (1941)

The mountain toward the west is Whitney. It marks the tallest point in the Sierra Nevadas, as well as the continental United States. From where I am camped, in the Alabama Hills ten miles to the east, Mount Whitney rises two miles into the atmosphere. It is evening and the mountain has begun to take on some of the color of the November sky, a frosty twilight blue like the color of a juniper berry or a piece of tinted glass that has been in the river a long time. Even as I watch, the finer details of the mountain are fading from view. Gradually the mass of rock grows simpler and simpler. After a few moments all that remains are a series of triangles, each a mile or so at the base, culminating in the jagged crest of the escarpment. On the summit the highest rocks are broken into vertical formations, each shaped like a spearhead. I can see now that there are patches of snow in the crevices near the top of the mountain, and that they reflect the color of the sky.

Down below, where I am camped, the air is still. There is no sound. There is no movement. Not one cricket chirps. Not one leaf moves. This is the edge of the vast desert that begins in Death Valley, that ranges as far north as Mono Lake, and that sprawls south as far as Joshua Tree. It is a dry country, with little more than sagebrush and bunch grass, bitterbrush, and beavertail cactus. Everywhere there are rocks, huge rounded boulders made of the same granite as the mountain, ranging in size from something on the order of a country church to a little one the size of an elephant. The Alabama Hills present a scene like so many in the Southwest, a spare austere country with dusty streambeds and big mountains, deer tracks and coyote spoor, fine-grained sand and cactus needles and weathered rocks. It is a land of concentrated beauty, a country best seen not from inside an automobile or from the height of a horse, but on foot and up close.

This is a landscape that, like so many other filming locations, resonates with associations both personal and cultural. As a little boy I watched *The Lone Ranger* on television every afternoon, putting my toys aside for awhile to enjoy the exploits of the masked superhero. Not half a mile from where I sit *The Lone Ranger* series was shot. From this point I can make out Lone Ranger Rock, Lone Ranger Canyon, Lone Ranger Ambush Site. On one of my first college dates I escorted a young lady to the annual Bogart festival at the campus auditorium and we watched a vintage black-and-white film from 1941 entitled *High Sierra*. That film was shot in the rock outcroppings directly in front of me. Humphrey Bogart was Mad Dog Earle, a doomed killer with a kind heart, and across those rocks in the distance he scrambled for the safety of the mountain fastness. Just to the south, in the rocks near Tuttle Creek, the Sierra Nevadas were transformed into the mountains of India for such classics as *Gunga Din, The Lives of a Bengal Lancer,* and *The Charge of the Light Brigade*. Even tonight filming goes on in these hills as the Disney people, camped a mile below me, are shooting background for an animated dinosaur movie.

The light grows dim and a faint breeze stirs, the first all day, as the last warmth of the earth rises into the heavens.

I recall the host of actors who have performed in these Alabama Hills—Tom Mix and Gene Autry, William Boyd and Douglas Fairbanks, Errol Flynn and Cary Grant, Tyrone Power and Gary Cooper, Spencer Tracy and John Wayne. They were all here once, the good, the bad, and the ugly, with their cameras and recording equipment, and now they are gone. All that remains is the timeless art they created, and the eternal landscape that inspired them.

What would they say if they could return from the grave?

Only the wind knows, the cold wind pouring down the slopes from Mount Whitney, the wind with the smell of snow on it, and it is not saying.

Stars twinkle. Coyotes sing. Darkness falls.

It occurs to me as I settle into the down sleeping bag—the same that has sheltered me in wilderness camps from northern Alaska to southern Arizona—that this place, the Alabama Hills, is a national treasure. Like so many of the other filming areas I have viewed on this journey—Professor Valley, Spanish Valley, Sevenmile Canyon, Mexican Hat, Valley of the Gods, Monument Valley, Old Pariah—it merits special commemoration and protection. It seems to me now, as it has at several other moments along the way, that the best way to preserve these areas is for a series of National Film Heritage Sites to be designated at selected locations across the country. Each location, and this would include sites in all regions of the country, would have a stone marker and bronze plaque. These stone markers would symbolize our national commitment to preserving areas essential to our artistic heritage and to educating the public about our cultural landscape.

Posterity will watch our films as the crowning artistic achievement of our age, as we now watch performances of Greek tragedy or Elizabethan drama. They will view these landscapes in the theater, and will want to return to view them in nature. It would be truly wonderful if they could still come out from the city and see the same undisturbed beauty that I view tonight.

NATURAL STATE

CALIFORNIA

The popular image of southern California is of gridlocked freeways, oppressive smog, and urban sprawl. A realm where hedonism has been elevated to the stature of a philosophical school, and vanity mirrors are the chief artifact of a minor religion. Where pit bulls rule the side streets and gun-toting teenagers prove Nobel-laureate William Golding was right when he wrote *Lord of the Flies*. Where various unpredictable natural disasters—forest fires, flash floods, mud slides, earthquakes, insect infestations—provide the general nihilistic atmosphere of an American Pompeii waiting to happen. For many thousands of square miles along the coast, this is the congested, dyspeptic, and unquiet state of affairs. Drive an hour or so from the city, though, and in virtually any direction, and you will be transported to another world: seacoasts as lovely as anything in Greece, mountains that evoke the Himalayas, forests with trees the height of twenty-story buildings, desert dune fields that bring to mind the Sahara, and prairies that fill with yellow and orange poppies every spring.

Since the beginning of film the wild landscapes of southern California have provided the setting for literally thousands of films. Here is the place where film was born, where it took its first hesitant steps, where it experienced a turbulent adolescence, and where it slowly matured into a universal art form of rare power and grace. Here, too, is the location where the new art form of television was created and almost overnight became the dominant form of media in world culture. For these reasons Los Angeles, the semi-mythic "City of Angels," has often been called the "entertainment capital of the world." There is no other place in the Southwestern region, not to mention the world, where so much that relates to film can be seen in so short a time.

Santa Monica National Recreation Area

Few areas have been as important to the development of motion pictures as the historic film ranches of the Santa Monica Mountains. In this scenic upland area, which is only an hour's drive north from the Los Angeles studios, hundreds of major and minor films and television programs have been shot over the decades. The park, which has been administered by the National Park Service since 1978, contains a patchwork of 70,000 acres of city, county, state, and federal lands. Protected areas include forested uplands, stream basins, grasslands, beaches, historic sites, and scenic overlooks. Historically, the area is part of a coastal landscape once dominated by Spanish (Franciscan) missions and colonial cattle ranches. Biologists consider the Santa Monica Mountains National Recreation Area to be a rare "living island" of native Southern California chaparral, oak woodlands, marshes, salt lagoons, and tidepools.

OPPOSITE: *Big Sur's clear skies, golden coasts, and turquoise waters help to make California the world's filmmaking capital. Courtesy John Murray.*

The Paramount Ranch in the Santa Monica National Recreation Area was used for several dozen films including THE VIRGINIAN *(Paramount, 1929) and the* GUNFIGHT AT THE O.K. CORRAL *(Paramount, 1957). Courtesy John Murray.*

Filmmakers have used the Santa Monica Mountains to create motion pictures since the earliest days of Hollywood. Major studios, most notably Paramount Pictures, owned movie ranches throughout the area. This process began in 1927, when Paramount purchased 2,400 acres of the old Rancho Las Virgenes. The ranch has since been used for dozens of films, featuring directors of the stature of Cecil B. DeMille and John Ford, and actors of the caliber of Gary Cooper, W. C. Fields, Dorothy Gish, Marlene Dietrich, Fay Wray, Lionel Barrymore, Cary Grant, Bing Crosby, Fred MacMurray, Henry Fonda, Walter Brennan, Bob Hope, John Wayne, Maureen O'Hara, Glenn Ford, Warren Beatty, and Diane Keaton. Such well known films as *The Adventures of Marco Polo, Wolf Song, The Santa Fe Trail, The Adventures of Tom Sawyer, A Farewell to Arms, The Plainsman, Wells Fargo, The Virginian, Gunfight at the O.K. Corral,* and *Reds* (which won a best directing Academy Award

for Warren Beatty) were shot either wholly or significantly on the ranch.

The "golden era" of filming at Paramount Ranch ended in the early 1950s when large-scale changes in the movie industry (most importantly, new competition from television) forced Paramount to sell the ranch. Following that, it changed ownership several times (coming into the public domain in 1980) but still continued to be used for filming and for television series (most notably, *Rin-Tin-Tin; The Rifleman; Have Gun Will Travel; Little House on the Prairie; The Dukes of Hazzard; Charlie's Angels; M*A*S*H; and Dr. Quinn, Medicine Woman*). The ranch continues to be used for filming. In fact, shortly before the author of this book toured the ranch in November of 1998, NBC filmed a made-for-television movie on the Woodstock concert of 1968 at the Paramount location (the actual event took place in Woodstock, New York).

The Paramount Ranch is open daily and is located on the Mulholland Highway about 4 miles west of the intersection with the Malibu Canyon/Las Virgenes Road. Most people who visit the historic filming ranch focus their attention on the western town, which anyone who ever watched Michael Landon's program *Little House on the Prairie* or *Dr. Quinn, Medicine Woman* will instantly recognize. The park service maintains a number of good hiking and riding trails in the area. Rangers regularly lead tours through the area, some of which focus on the rich film and television history of the region.

Another area of importance to film and television in the Santa Monica Mountains is Malibu Creek State Park, which preserves a drainage of around 6,600 acres in the middle of the range. Most of the internal park roads follow Malibu Creek, which meanders roughly from west to east through the area. The long-running television series *M*A*S*H* was sometimes shot in the park. Local orientation maps, natural history literature, and directions for ranger-guided tours can be obtained at the state park district headquarters, which is located near the intersection of Malibu Canyon Road and Mulholland Highway.

OPPOSITE: *In John Sturges'* GUNFIGHT AT THE O.K. CORRAL *(Paramount, 1957), Burt Lancaster as Wyatt Earp faces down the Clanton Gang in the streets of Tombstone. Courtesy Eddie Brandt's Saturday Matinee.*

Gunfight at the O.K. Corral

This 1957 re-telling of the Doc Holliday–Wyatt Earp battle with the Clanton Gang featured a cast of future Oscar-winning actors, including Burt Lancaster (Wyatt Earp), Kirk Douglas (Doc Holliday), and Dennis Hopper (Billy Clanton). Filmed partially on the Paramount Ranch, with a script written by novelist Leon Uris, *Gunfight at the O.K. Corral* was directed by John Sturges, whose previous credits included *Bad Day at Black Rock* (1955) with Spencer Tracy. Sturges would go on to direct Spencer Tracy again in *The Old Man and the Sea* (1958). In later films, including *The Magnificent Seven* (1960) and *The Great Escape* (1963), Sturges would establish himself as one of the premier directors of the fast-paced action movie in the twentieth century. An exacting craftsman, Sturges took forty-four hours to film the five-minute shoot-out that provides the culminating scene for *Gunfight at the O.K. Corral*. The film grossed nearly $5 million, which was considered a fortune in the late 1950s. Like most westerns, *Gunfight at the O.K. Corral* was shot at several locations, including the Paramount Ranch, Tombstone, and Tucson (Old Tucson film set). This is one of the classic "law versus outlaw" stories of the Southwest. No finer ensemble of actors has ever attempted to tell this famous tale of the old frontier.

ALABAMA HILLS

The Alabama Hills area is one of the most popular filming locations in the country. Part of the attraction is the spectacular backdrop of Mount Whitney, the highest mountain in the Lower 48, rising to 14,494 feet above the surrounding landscape of the Owens River Valley. The area is distinguished by thousands of rounded granite outcrops and enormous boulders scattered over the rolling lowlands. The combination of these two unique geological features provides cinematographers with the best of both worlds—a scenic, four-season desert area only 6 miles from the dramatic snow-capped peaks of the High Sierras. Add to this a convenient network of dirt access roads, a short four-hour drive from the studios of Los Angeles, a friendly support town just a few minutes down the road (Lone Pine) and you have a near-perfect filming location. In fact, since the beginning of film, the Alabama Hills area has been used in over 150 films and about a dozen television series, and continues to be used actively in the twenty-first century.

Geologists tell us that the Owens River Valley is a graben (a German word for "ditch") between two fault-block mountain ranges: the towering Sierra Nevadas to the west and the much lower Inyo Mountains to the east. Because of its close proximity to major continental faults, the Owens River Valley, which includes the Alabama Hills, has often experienced the destructive effects of powerful earthquakes. The great Lone Pine earthquake of March 26, 1872, measured over 8 on the Richter scale, putting it on the level of the 1906 earthquake that devastated San Francisco. In fact, a significant remnant of that quake—a fifteen- to twenty-foot-high fault scarp (exposed ridge)—can be seen running north to south through the Alabama Hills.

Most of the rocks in the Alabama Hills are older volcanic and granitic rocks and are typically colored brown, orange, and gray. Deeply weathered, they contrast starkly with the sharp angles of the high alpine peaks. Although naturalists once believed—largely because of their solid, timeless appearance—that the rocks of the Alabama Hills were among "the oldest in the world," modern science has proven that the rocks are actually about the same age as the Sierra Nevadas—about 150 to 200 million years (contrast that with the 1.1 billion-year-old granite and greenstone of the truly ancient Blue Ridge Mountains in Virginia). These native Alabama Hill rock formations, though, have long provided a perfect landscape for movie actors to ambush stagecoaches, find refuge from marauding Indians, hide from the local authorities, and even fight the epic battles of colonial India.

Film historians believe that as early as 1920 silent movies were being made in the Alabama Hills. One of the earliest was the 1925 Tom Mix picture *Riders of the Purple Sage*, which was based on the Zane Grey novel of the same title. A few years later a very young John Wayne, wearing that distinctive white scarf, along with the rest of his "Singing Riders" made one of his forgettable early pictures here: *Westward Ho*.

Movie actors have been ambushing stagecoaches and hiding from marauding Indians for years in the Alabama Hills. Courtesy John Murray.

Then came William Boyd (Hopalong Cassidy), who filmed several dozen of his popular cowboy pictures in the Alabama Hills. The rest, as they say, has been the stuff of history: *Lives of a Bengal Lancer,* with Gary Cooper in 1935; *Gunga Din*, with Douglas Fairbanks in 1939; *Yellow Sky*, with Gregory Peck and Anne Baxter in 1948; *Bad Day at Black Rock*, with Spencer Tracy in 1955; *How the West Was Won*, with Jimmy Stewart and George Peppard in 1962; and countless others. It was in the Alabama Hills in 1979, just a few months before his death, that John Wayne did his last bit of acting in a television commercial for Western Federal Savings and Loan. More recently, the Alabama Hills area has been seen in films as diverse as *Star Trek V* (1989) and *Tremors* (1989).

The Alabama Hills are located just west of Lone Pine, which is found along U.S. 395 south of Manzanar. Access to the 30,000-acre natural area, which is managed by the Bureau of Land Management to permanently preserve its scenic values, is easy—just follow the Whitney Portal Road west from the center of Lone Pine for about 2.7 miles. Then take a right at Movie Road, which is marked with a large bronze memorial. The landscape accessed by Movie Road can be separated into two distinct areas: the extensive rock formations just east of it and the canyon-cut flats to the northwest (which can be reached by taking the left fork when the road divides). In the former area visitors can find many of the locations where, among others, the film *Yellow Sky* was shot. This is also the region where Gary Cooper Rock, Gene Autry Rock, Lone Ranger Canyon and Hopalong Cassidy Ambush Rock can be found (all marked plainly on the BLM map). The canyon-cut flat contains areas used in *High Sierra, Gunga Din, Rawhide, Charge of the Light Brigade, How the West Was Won*, and various Gene Autry and Roy Rogers films.

Orientation maps for the Alabama Hills, and additional recreational information, can be obtained at the BLM high desert office on

U.S. 395, one mile south of town. A good BLM campground with about fifty sites can be found along Tuttle Creek a few miles south of the Alabama Hills (accessed by Whitney Portal Road—take a left on Horseshoe Meadow Road and head south about 2.5 miles). Anyone visiting the Alabama Hills should follow the Whitney Portal Road all the way into the mountains, and view up close the splendor of the High Sierras.

Joe Kidd

Joe Kidd (1972) is one of the better films made in the Alabama Hills, in terms of its aesthetic use of the landscape. It was also among the group of transitional films made by actor Clint Eastwood, as he moved from the spaghetti-Westerns of Italian film director Sergio Leone—*A Fistful of Dollars* (1964); *For A Few Dollars More* (1965); *The Good, the Bad, and the Ugly* (1966)—back into the more familiar landscapes of the American West (a region in which he would, a quarter of a century later, make his Oscar-winning Western, *The Unforgiven*). *Joe Kidd* shows how much Eastwood learned from the Italian master. Although the opening and closing scenes of *Joe Kidd* were shot at the Old Tucson film set west of Tucson, Arizona, the vast bulk of the film, and all of the key character-development sequences, were shot in the Alabama Hills.

In the film, which was written by Elmore Leonard, Eastwood plays a small-time rancher named Joe Kidd who, when we first meet him, has been thrown into the local jail for public drunkenness. Dressed in unlikely attire—a bowler derby and worn-down vested suit—Eastwood at first seems an unlikely candidate for his primary role in the story (gunfighter). Shortly thereafter, though, Robert Duvall, a frontier land baron, enters town with a motley entourage of hired shooters. Duvall is looking for a local guide to help him hunt a Mexican land-reformer who is threatening his property. He pays Eastwood's fine on the condition that Eastwood work for him. Although Eastwood initially signs on with Duvall, he eventually becomes disgusted with himself and the evil nature of his benefactor, and switches sides. This script, with its subversive

Clint Eastwood as Joe Kidd fights an unscrupulous land baron and his henchmen in John Sturges' JOE KIDD *(Universal, 1972). Courtesy Eddie Brandt's Saturday Matinee.*

theme, fits in perfectly not only with Eastwood's typical westerns—in which he is fighting for the underdog and the victims of injustice—but also with his many contemporary crime films (in which, similarly, he allies himself with the downtrodden and sinned-against and tirelessly does battle against corrupt individuals and institutions).

Major sequences of *Joe Kidd* were shot in the extensive rock formations just east of Movie Road, as well as on the sage flats to the west of Horseshoe Meadow Road, which runs due south from Whitney Portal Road.

Gary Cooper

Before there was Humphrey Bogart, before there was John Wayne, before there was Clint Eastwood, there was Gary Cooper (1901–1960)—the ultimate model for all actors who have aspired to play the strong, silent hero. The son of a Montana Supreme Court justice, Cooper learned from his father at an early age the old frontier virtues of personal strength and public reticence, and these qualities would later become his acting trademark. After attending college (Wesleyan and Grinnell), Cooper worked briefly as a ranger in Yellowstone National Park and then set off for the bright lights of Hollywood. Within a few years he was regularly playing minor cowboy roles in Westerns, appearing in such pictures as *The Vanishing American* and *Wild Horse Mesa*. Every successful career must have its lucky break, and Cooper's was a second lead in *The Winning of Barbara Worth* (1926), a now-forgotten film that was a box-office hit during the Roaring Twenties.

From there, Cooper's career blossomed, as he appeared in film after film, sometimes starring in as many two or three a year (*Wolf Song, Betrayal, The Virginian*—1929). His relaxed manner, laconic delivery, and quiet self-confidence became the screen presence most imitated by other male actors during the Great Depression and War years. In 1942, Cooper received an Oscar for his performance in *Sergeant York*. In 1952, he received another Oscar for *High Noon*, perhaps his finest film. (Shot in central California, *High Noon* also helped to launch the careers of such actors as Grace Kelly and Lloyd Bridges). A third Oscar for life-time achievement followed in 1960, two months before his death from cancer.

Many of Cooper's films were shot in the Southwest, particularly in the Alabama Hills below Mount Whitney *(Lives of a Bengal Lancer, Springfield Rifle)*. The roles he played embodied the best in the American character—courage, optimism, generosity, personal integrity, reverence for life—and his career will forever be associated with the West he so dearly loved.

Gary Cooper as lawman Will Kane protects an undeserving community and is the man alone in Fred Zinneman's HIGH NOON *(UA, 1952). Courtesy Eddie Brandt's Saturday Matinee.*

Death Valley National Park

Death Valley National Park is another one of those southern California locations, like the Santa Monica Mountains or the Alabama Hills, that has seen heavy location shooting since the beginning of film. The reasons are simple: a wonderful diversity of desert landscapes, over three hundred days of sunlight annually, good shooting weather in the winter months, and close proximity to the Los Angeles studios. The park contains the lowest elevation in North America (-282 feet at Badwater) as well as 11,049-foot Telescope Peak. In Death Valley (which is the largest national park in the continental United States) there are salt flats that stretch for miles (perfect, in ages past, for high-speed chase scenes involving stagecoaches and Indians on horseback), broad regions of sand dunes (excellent for outer-space movies), volcanic craters, ancient marble canyons, impressive geological overlooks (as in Dante's View), brilliantly hued rock cliffs, colorful historical sites (particularly pertaining to the early mining period), and vast stretches of open creosote desert. Death Valley is a place like no other in the Southwest, and, unlike many other areas in the country, is at its very best during the ordinarily inclement months of December and January. This is the special area first made famous by Mary Austin's book *The Land of Little Rain* (1903) and later immortalized in the black-and-white landscape photographs of Ansel Adams.

The films that have been made in Death Valley include virtually every genre: *Greed* (1925), *20 Mule Team* (1940), *Spartacus* (1960), *The Greatest Story Ever Told* (1965), *The Professionals* (1966), *Star Wars* (1977), *Revenge of the Jedi* (1983), and *The Doors* (1991). Television shows have also been shot in Death Valley, including Ronald Reagan's *Death Valley Days* (1950s) and Rod Sterling's *The Twilight Zone* (1959). The most popular shooting locations have traditionally been within a thirty-mile radius of Furnace Creek. They include Badwater Basin (where the old mule teams made their pull in *20 Mule Team*), the sand dunes of Stovepipe Wells (seen in the early silent *Greed*, as well as in *Star Wars*), Dante's View (where Luke and Obi-Wan look down on the

The sand dunes of Stovepipe Wells in Death Valley National Park were seen in STAR WARS *(20th-Fox, 1977). Courtesy John Murray.*

OPPOSITE: *Mark Hamill (Luke Skywalker), Alec Guiness (Obi-Wan Kenobi), Anthony Daniels (C-3PO), and Kenny Baker (R2-D2) in George Lucas'* STAR WARS *(20th-Fox, 1977). Courtesy Eddie Brandt's Saturday Matinee.*

desolate frontier outpost in *Star Wars*), and Mushroom Rock Canyon south of Furnace Creek (where Luke uses his binoculars to scan the landscape in *Star Wars*). These are all beautiful locations, and are easily accessible from the road system around the Furnace Creek visitor center. One other filming site of note in the Death Valley area is the state-managed Trona Pinnacles, which can be found ten miles south of Trona via State Route 178. The site appeared in *Star Trek V.*

It is unlikely that Death Valley National Park will continue to be utilized as it has been for filmmaking because of the environmental restrictions that were imposed by the California Desert Protection Act of 1994. Much of the park is now designated as wilderness. As a result, most off-road shooting is no longer possible. Filmmakers have shifted to other areas of the Mojave Desert, particularly Bureau of Land Management land, where there are fewer permit restrictions. Still, the Death Valley landscape will forever resonate with associations from the great age of filmmaking in the twentieth century. Here audiences saw early silent films that modestly recalled the old frontier as well as ambitious modern space epics that provided a dazzling glimpse of the distant future.

Mono Lake

Mono Lake is located in a vast arid basin (the Mono Basin) that is a province of the Great Basin Desert (the large intermountain desert just to the north of the much smaller Mojave Desert). To the west of Mono Lake are some of the most striking mountains of the Sierras, a segment of them within the boundaries of Yosemite National Park. The enormous alkaline lake, which is part of a once-active volcanic landscape, is surrounded by public domain, most of it administered by the Bureau of Land Management and the Forest Service (Inyo National Forest). Perhaps the best description of the unique Mono Lake region was made by Mark Twain, who passed through it after the Civil War:

Mono Lake lies in a lifeless, treeless, hideous desert, eight thousand feet above the level of the sea, and is guarded by mountains two thousand feet higher, whose summits are always clothed in clouds. This solemn, silent, sailess sea—this lonely tenant of the loneliest spot on earth—is little graced with the picturesque. It is an unpretending expanse of grayish water, about a hundred miles in circumference, with two islands in its center, mere upheavals of rent and scorched and blistered lava, snowed over with gray banks and drifts of pumice stone and ashes, the winding sheet of the dead volcano, whose vast crater the lake has seized upon and occupied.

The Mono Lake area is popular for filmmaking because of its striking high-desert setting, dramatic mountain ranges, and ample public land. Access to one of the more popular filming areas—the south shore of Mono Lake near Paoha Island (where much of *High Plains Drifter* was shot)—is provided by State Route 120, which branches to the northeast from U.S. 395 north of Lee Vining (drive east on State Route 120 about 5.1 miles—the filming location is to the north along the lake shore). The 10-mile stretch of U.S. 395 between Lee Vining and June Lake Junction, near Mono Lake, also provides superb views of Mono Lake and the famous Mono Domes (large volcanic domes comprised of rhyolitic glass and pumice).

High Plains Drifter
It was the singular physical qualities of Mono Lake—a purgatorial landscape that seems to embody all that is evoked by the word desolation—that brought actor/director Clint Eastwood to the location in 1972. Once there, he would shoot one of his most compelling films, *High Plains Drifter.* The film, which grossed over $7 million (a great

Clint Eastwood

Clint Eastwood was born on May 31, 1930, in San Francisco. Like many children of the Great Depression, Eastwood grew up in poverty. After graduating from high school he worked at a number of menial jobs and eventually attended Los Angeles City College. By the mid-1950s he had somehow worked himself into the bottom ranks of the film industry, finding the occasional bit part. Even in these early, forgettable films—*Revenge of the Creature, Francis in the Navy, Tarantula*—audiences watching late-night cable can occasionally glimpse the beginnings of the mature character player. Throughout this period Eastwood had to work outside the film industry (most often as a swimming pool installer) to support his family. Eastwood's first major break came in the television series *Rawhide*, which ran for eight seasons from 1958 through 1964. Eastwood played a minor character named Rowdy Yates.

In terms of Southwestern landscapes, several films in Eastwood's lengthy life-list stand out. The first is *Hang 'Em High* (1968), which made effective use of White Sands National Monument in southern New Mexico. The next is *Joe Kidd* (1972), which was filmed in the Alabama Hills below Mount Whitney in California and at the Old Tucson film set in southern Arizona. Another of Eastwood's classics—*High Plains Drifter*—was shot at Mono Lake in California. *High Plains Drifter* appeared a year after *Joe Kidd* and featured Eastwood's directorial debut. It is his most pure film in what have come to be known as Eastwood themes (the wronged man fighting for personal justice, the moral individual versus the corrupt system, the immense desert landscape as a looming backdrop for intense human drama). Four years later, Eastwood both acted in and directed another Western classic, *The Outlaw Josey Wales*, which was shot at the Old Pariah film set near Page. A final Eastwood film that made significant use of the Southwestern landscape was *The Eiger Sanction* (1975), shot partially at Zion National Park and in Monument Valley. Eastwood also directed that film.

Just when everyone thought that Eastwood would never make another Western, he surprised us all and produced his greatest work in the genre. *The Unforgiven*, shot outside the Southwest, swept the Oscars in 1992 with awards for best picture, best director (Eastwood), and best actor (Gene Hackman). In the film Eastwood plays a gunfighter hired by a group of prostitutes to seek revenge on an outlaw who has grievously injured one of them. Eastwood is the finest practitioner of the genre—both as an actor and director—since the "Golden Age" of John Wayne and John Ford.

Many of Clint Eastwood's characters follow the theme of pursuing justice. Courtesy Photofest.

success at the time), accurately reflected the national mood of the early 1970s. Within the previous four years, the nation had been shocked and in some cases literally torn apart by a series of traumatic events: two political assassinations (Senator Robert Kennedy and Reverend Martin Luther King), the worsening crisis of the Vietnam War (the 1968 My Lai Massacre, the 1971 bombing of Cambodia), almost weekly campus demonstrations (some of which turned violent), and widespread urban riots (Newark, Detroit, Chicago, Los Angeles). The national mood was one of cynicism and despair, and this was most clearly reflected in the music world: the Rolling Stones concert at Altamont, California (which erupted into a violent melee); the final breakup of the Beatles; the drug-overdose deaths of Jim Morrison, Jimi Hendrix, and Janis Joplin; and a new sadness and world-weariness in popular songs.

High Plains Drifter is best seen in this turbulent cultural context. With its bleak outlook and explosive violence, the film provided a perfect metaphor for the widespread pessimism of the period. This probably explains, in part, its unexpected success (similar to that of *Stagecoach* in 1939, or *The Searchers* in 1956, which also provided an allegory for the nation's mood at an axial moment in history).

The film has an unusual plot for a western. It is the story of a federal marshal who is killed by a gang of local bullies (with the townspeople meekly looking on). The marshal then returns from the grave to exact revenge on both the gang and the town (Largo). This is a tale—part fantasy and part reality—that could have been written by Ambrose Bierce ("An Occurrence at Owl Creek Bridge") or Stephen Crane ("A Man and Some Others"), and yet it is also uniquely modern in its message.

One thing is clear as soon as Clint Eastwood (the living ghost of Marshal Jim Duncan) steps onto the screen—the man who had former-ly portrayed Rowdy Yates in the TV Western series *Rawhide* had learned volumes about both acting and directing while working on those three spaghetti-Westerns with acclaimed Italian director Sergio Leone. Eastwood had, like Gary Cooper and John Wayne before him, after years of hard work, finally mastered a slow-moving, understated acting presence that conveyed great power on the screen. In addition to starring in the film, Eastwood also directed the production.

Unlike most westerns, *High Plains Drifter* was shot entirely at a single location—the shores of Mono Lake near Paoha Island (see above for directions). This is one of those rare films in which the landscape, because of the continuity of the shooting, becomes a strong presence and, eventually, an essential character in the story. One senses in the long, brooding shots of the barren desert flats, brilliant alkaline water, and distant blue mountains that the real force exacting revenge on the people of Largo is nature (in the same sense expressed by Aeschylus in his often-quoted line: "Those who the gods will destroy they first make mad with power").

Certainly one of the most haunting moments in the history of the western occurs in the final scene of *High Plains Drifter*, when Clint Eastwood, on his way out of town, rides past the Largo cemetery. The dwarf Mordecai Fortusse (portrayed superbly by Billy Curtis) is carving a name (Marshal Jim Duncan) on a wooden cross. He looks up at Eastwood and says, "By the way, stranger, I never did know your name." Eastwood gives him one of those classic narrow-eyed squints and quietly replies, "Yes, you do." The reaction shot records the horrified look on Mordecai's face as he realizes he is staring at the spirit of Marshal Jim Duncan. A long lens shot then follows Clint Eastwood/Marshal Duncan on horseback as he disappears into the heat haze of the Mono Lake desert—a perfect ending for a film that took a lot of risks and succeeded.

OPPOSITE: *Verna Bloom as Sarah Belding and Clint Eastwood as the living ghost of Marshal Jim Duncan reflect the turbulence and despair of the 1960s and 1970s in Clint Eastwood's* HIGH PLAINS DRIFTER *(Universal, 1972). Courtesy Eddie Brandt's Saturday Matinee.*

Gene Autry

Gene Autry, born in Tioga, Texas, on September 29, 1907, was the son of a tenant farmer. He was working as a railroad telegrapher in Oklahoma when Will Rogers just happened to hear him sing and suggested he enter show business. Within a few months Autry was making his first studio recordings and singing on local radio stations. Eventually, like many people during the Great Depression years, he moved west to Los Angeles. In 1934, Autry made his first appearance in a film *(In Old Santa Fe)*. After a brief stint in a minor serial *(Phantom Empire)*, Autry was given a starring role in a major production *(Tumblin' Tumbleweeds, 1934)*. This soon led to literally dozens of films for Republic Pictures *(South of the Border, Rancho Grande, Down Mexico Way)*. Autry regularly appeared with his comic partner, Smiley Burnette, and his favorite horse, Champion. Although most of his films were shot in the Alabama Hills near Mount Whitney, Autry also worked quite often on studio land in the hills and valleys north of Los Angeles.

Autry perfected the role of the strong, virtuous cowboy combating evil in the Old West, a character type that has been parodied in such films as *Three Amigos!* (Steve Martin, Chevy Chase, Martin Short). For his part, Autry laughed all the way to bank. For years he was the only Western actor to be listed among the top ten moneymakers in Hollywood films (1938–1942). He also wrote over two hundred songs, including such popular favorites as "Back in the Saddle Again" and "Here Comes Santa Claus." A brilliant entrepreneur, Autry went on to own a chain of radio and television stations (one of his stations, KTLA in Los Angeles, sold for $245 million in 1982), cattle ranches (the largest spread, a 20,000-acre cattle ranch in Arizona), oil fields, various corporations, half a dozen major hotels, and, his favorite, the California Angels baseball team.

In 1988, Gene Autry opened the Autry Museum of Western Heritage near Griffith Park in Los Angeles. Among the items in the $54 million facility are an antique fire engine from Nevada, guns owned by Wyatt Earp and Annie Oakley, and numerous exhibits and displays featuring different periods in the development of the West. Autry died at his home in Studio City on October 2, 1998, at the age of 91, one of the most remarkable figures in the history of American cinema.

Gene Autry perfected the role of the strong, virtuous cowboy in the Old West. Courtesy Eddie Brandt's Saturday Matinee.

Algodones Dune Fields

The Algodones Dune Fields, in the extreme southeast corner of California, comprise one of the largest open-dune systems in the United States. About forty miles long and just to the west of the Colorado River valley, the dune field ranges from six to eight miles in width. Because of the good access roads, ample sunshine (336 sunny days per year), and strikingly beautiful desert scenery, the "Sand Hills," as they are called by locals, have been used regularly for filmmaking since the 1920s. Films shot on the sand dunes include *The Sheik* (1926), *The Lost Patrol* (1934), *Suez* (1938), *Sahara* (1943), *The Desert Fox* (1951), *Tobruk* (1967), *The Getaway* (1994), and *Stargate* (1994). Television series shot on the dunes include *Rat Patrol*. Additionally, the dunes are often used for commercial advertising (everything from automobiles to fashion shoots).

The dune fields (68,700 acres) are managed by the Bureau of Land Management. They are crossed by California Highway 78 to the north and by Interstate 8 to the south. Most filming has been done at sites accessed by California Highway 78. The dune fields are a great area for winter camping and recreation (as with Death Valley, though, they are too hot in the summer months).

Other Locations in Southern California

Notable shooting locations for every variety of film (and television) abound across the landscape of southern California, and are often readily accessible to the general public. What follows are a few of the more popular and historic locations, in roughly geographic order from the Monterey area south along the coast to San Diego, along with assorted other sites of compelling interest to Southwest film aficionados.

Point Lobos State Reserve (4 miles south of Carmel on Highway 1, Monterey)—This unique Pacific coastal park, made famous by the black-and-white landscape photographs of local residents Edward Weston and Ansel Adams, has served as a primary shooting location for a number of films. These include such popular movies as *The Sandpiper* (1964) and *The Graduate* (1967). In *The Sandpiper*, written by Oscar-winner Dalton Trumbo (see *Lonely Are the Brave*, New Mexico), Elizabeth Taylor starred as a nonconformist artistic-type who was involved in a love triangle with Richard Burton and Eva Marie Saint (husband and wife in the film). The dramatically beautiful Big Sur coast provided the perfect backdrop for the romantic film, which also spawned the Oscar-winning theme song, "The Shadow of Your Smile." The Big Sur area also played a prominent role in several films of the 1940s, most notably Alfred Hitchcock's *Rebecca* (1940), which starred Sir Laurence Olivier and won Oscars for best picture and for Cinematography, and *Lassie Come Home* (1943), which featured an eleven-year-old Elizabeth Taylor and a fifteen-year-old Roddy McDowall.

Monterey Bay Aquarium (886 Cannery Row, Monterey)—This is the same aquarium that Captain Kirk (William Shatner) and Mister Spock (Leonard Nimoy) visited in the 1986 film *Star Trek IV: The Voyage Home*. In fact, the entire plot was premised on their bringing a mated pair of humpbacked whales back to the twenty-third century. The scene in which Mister Spock swims with a whale, performing a cross-species Vulcan mind-meld, was shot in the Kelp Forest Exhibit, an enormous, thirty-foot-high aquarium featuring marine life common to the off-shore California kelp beds.

Garrapatta State Beach (just south of the Carmel Highlands off Highway 1, Monterey)—This state park served as the location for the beach scene in the 1993 film *Basic Instinct*, in which Michael Douglas portrays a police officer attempting to prove that Sharon Stone has committed a homicide.

William Asher's BIKINI BEACH *(American Int., 1964) is the third installment of beach films starring Frankie Avalon as Frankie and Annette Funicello as Dee Dee. Courtesy Eddie Brandt's Saturday Matinee.*

SANTA CRUZ BOARDWALK (400 Beach Street, Santa Cruz)—Clint Eastwood fans will recognize the Coconut Grove Ballroom, on the Santa Cruz boardwalk, as the location where Dirty Harry (Eastwood) causes a gangster to have a heart attack in the 1983 film *Sudden Impact*. The final scene of the film, with typical Eastwood vengeance, takes place on the park's carousel ride.

PARADISE COVE (28100 block of Pacific Coast Highway, Malibu)— Just thirty minutes up the Pacific Coast Highway from Santa Monica is the lovely surfing beach that will forever be associated with the legendary film careers of former-Mouseketeers Frankie Avalon and Annette Funicello. It was Paradise Cove that served as the location for a whole cottage industry of beach movies during the 1960s, as in *Beach Party* (1963), *Bikini Beach* (1964), and *Beach Blanket Bingo* (1965). These films can still be seen regularly on Ted Turner's AMC cable channel. Occasional guest appearances by such old-school comedians as Don Rickles and Paul Lynde make these light-hearted films even more enjoyable.

HYATT REGENCY BEACH (200 South Pine Avenue, Long Beach)— All those who liked Arnold Schwarzenegger's 1993 film *Last Action Hero* will recognize this hotel. Some of the film's most entertaining scenes, including the one in which Arnold makes off with a corpse during a funeral, were shot at this location.

THE QUEEN MARY (Pier J at the end of the Long Beach Freeway)— This grand old ship appeared in literally dozens of films, including *The Poseidon Adventure* (1972).

GREYSTONE PARK AND MANSION (905 Loma Vista Drive, Beverly Hills)—The Greystone, a fifty-plus–room mansion, was once the most sizable home in the exclusive enclave of Beverly Hills. Built by oil magnate Edward L. Doheny during the Roaring Twenties, the opulent palace has aged well and has appeared in such recent Hollywood standards as *Ghostbusters* (1984), *The Witches of Eastwick* (1987), *The Bodyguard* (1992), *Death Becomes Her* (1992), and *Indecent Proposal* (1993). The mansion has also been seen quite often on television in such long-running series as *Dynasty* and *Falcon Crest*.

REGENT BEVERLY WILSHIRE HOTEL (9500 Wilshire Boulevard, Beverly Hills)—This renowned establishment became even better known in 1990 with the release of *Pretty Woman*. The film explored an unlikely romance between a wealthy businessman (Richard Gere) who has just lost the father from whom he has been long estranged, and a lonely, struggling, good-hearted lady of the evening (Julia Roberts). It also introduced the public to another side of actor Jason Alexander, who would later achieve much recognition for his brilliant work on the popular sitcom *Seinfeld*.

GRIFFITH PARK OBSERVATORY (2800 East Observatory Road, Hollywood Hills)—Griffith Park (4,107 acres) is one of the jewels of Los Angeles, and compares favorably with some of the nicest urban parks in the United States, including Golden Gate Park in San Francisco and Central Park in New York. The park is located at the far eastern end of the Santa Monica Mountains. The park's astronomical dome, visible from Hollywood Boulevard (otherwise known as the combat zone), has appeared in two memorable films: *Rebel Without a Cause* (1955) and *The Terminator* (1984). In the James Dean film, the observatory was the location of the climactic fight scene at the end of the picture. A bronze bust of James Dean can be found along the walkway of the observatory. In the second film, the observatory served as the location where Arnold "The Time Traveler" Swarzenegger first arrived in the present era (sans clothing) as a computer droid sent from the future.

WESTIN BONAVENTURE HOTEL (404 South Figueroa Street, downtown LA)—Three contemporary films have utilized this futuristic-looking hotel: *Rain Man* (car salesman Tom Cruise meets there with

the executor of his father's estate), *True Lies* (federal agent Arnold Swarzenegger rides a police horse through the lobby, and then, via elevator, rides his mount out onto the roof), and *In the Line of Fire* (secret service officer Clint Eastwood tangles with would-be assassin John Malkovich in the exterior elevator).

BILTMORE HOTEL (506 South Grand Avenue, downtown LA)—The Biltmore is one of the oldest and most beautiful hotels in the city, dating back (like many of the finer buildings) to the ornate period of the 1920s. For nearly a decade, from 1931 through 1942, the Biltmore sponsored most of the annual Academy Award ceremonies. It was here, during the 1960 Democratic National Convention, that a forty-three-year old junior senator from Massachusetts (John F. Kennedy) maintained his busy headquarters. Several hundred films have utilized the hotel, including *Vertigo* (1958), *The Sting* (1973), and *Beverly Hills Cop* (1984). Few could stand straight-faced at the front desk and still recall the hilarious scene in *Beverly Hills Cop* in which Detroit police detective Axel Foley (Eddie Murphy) claims to be a reporter from *Rolling Stone* magazine about to interview pop singer/celebrity Michael Jackson.

BRADBURY BUILDING (304 South Broadway, downtown LA)—The Bradbury (now over a century old) has appeared in two films starring Jack Nicholson—*Chinatown* (1974) and *Wolf* (1994). The formidable office building, with its dramatic inner court, works well either as a law office or as a publishing house.

LOS ANGELES CITY HALL (200 North Spring Street, downtown LA)—The author of this book will always remember this distinctive structure as the headquarters of *The Daily Planet* in the 1950s television show *Superman*. More recently, City Hall has appeared in such films as *48 Hours* (1982) and *Dragnet* (1987). The building is also a regular fixture in television drama, appearing in everything from *Kojak* and *The Rockford Files* to *Matlock* and *L.A. Law*.

Studios and Museums

Autry Museum of Western Heritage (4700 Western
Heritage Way, Los Angeles)—The Autry Museum, which is adjacent to
Griffith Park, will be of interest to all aficionados of the classic Western
($7.50 in 2000). Autry was one of the giants of the film industry (as
well as one of the most successful businessmen in southern California).
The museum presents a history of America's westward movement and
its representation in film and television.

The Museum of Television and Radio in California
(465 North Beverly Drive, Beverly Hills)—Museum exhibits feature
the history of both media. Visitors ($6 in 2000) can use a computer
to select historic radio and television programs and enjoy them on
individual consoles.

NBC (300 West Alameda Avenue, Burbank)—The tour ($6 in 2000)
runs about 75 minutes and features stops at wardrobe, makeup, sound
effects, and other TV departments. It is still possible to sit in the audience
and observe a taping of that American cultural icon, *The Tonight Show.*

Paramount Studios (5555 Melrose Avenue, Hollywood)—One
of the better walking tours ($22 in 2000). Much film history was made
here. The opulent wrought-iron gate at the corner of Bronson Avenue
and Marathon Street (not the major entrance) has appeared in dozens
of films. The gate was shown in the opening credits for a popular television program, *Sunset Boulevard.*

Warner Brothers (4000 Warner Boulevard, Burbank)—The
tour ($30 in 2000) runs a couple of hours, is surprisingly thorough,
and is worth every penny. Warner limits its tours to smaller groups of
people, which allows for real questions and a real learning experience.
The tour sometimes includes live filming and always stops by the
Warner Brothers Museum (much historic film memorabilia). No cameras or tape recorders are permitted.

Universal Studios (100 Universal City Plaza, Universal City)—
Among other things, the tour ($36 in 2000) stops by the original Bates
Motel, which was featured in Alfred Hitchcock's masterpiece thriller
Psycho (1960). The series *Leave it to Beaver* (among many other fine programs) was filmed at this historic location. The elaborate tour, part of
which is on an aerial tram, includes demonstrations of special effects
and familiar sets from such blockbuster films as *E.T., Jurassic Park, Back
to the Future,* and *Backdraft.*

Hotel del Coronado (1500 Orange Avenue, Coronado)—This
scenic five-story beachfront hotel, painted zinc white and surrounded
by beautiful flower gardens and tall royal palm trees, was first featured
in the 1929 silent film *The Flying Fleet* (starring the blonde leading lady
of the period, Anita Page). Since then the Coronado was used most
notably as the Florida backdrop for Billy Wilder's classic romantic
comedy *Some Like It Hot* (1959), featuring Marilyn Monroe, Jack
Lemmon, and Tony Curtis. In the film, Lemmon and Curtis portray
two musicians who pretend to be women in Monroe's all-female revue
in order to elude Prohibition-era gangsters. More recently, *The Stunt
Man* (1978), an underrated dark comedy with Peter O'Toole in the lead
role, was filmed at the Coronado. O'Toole portrayed a film director
who offers to hide a fugitive (portrayed by Steve Railsback) on the set,
if he'll replace the stunt man who has been accidentally killed by
Railsback. This unusual arrangement makes for a lively narrative—and
a plot line, incidentally, which derives from "hidden character" comedies that were popular in Renaissance theater (Shakespeare) as well as
in ancient Roman drama (Seneca).

Anthony Perkins as Norman Bates is the troubled young manager of The Bates Motel in Alfred Hitchcock's PSYCHO *(Universal, 1960). Courtesy Eddie Brandt's Saturday Matinee.*

NEVADA

hree wonderful deserts are found in Nevada. They can be thought of as three sisters, each lovely and charming in its own way, but each pleasantly different from the other, in terms of character, mood, and physical appearance. First there is the Great Basin Desert, the largest desert in the United States, which runs from the northern part of the state south into Nye County. It is known for its sagebrush, prickly pear cactus, and free-ranging herds of wild horses. In the southwest corner of Nevada, basically in and around Las Vegas, we have the Mojave Desert, a much warmer desert noted for its unique, yucca-like Joshua trees. In the far southeastern corner of the state, along the drainage of the Colorado River, there is a small portion of the Painted Desert, which is most distinguished by its red sedimentary rock. This is the area of Hoover Dam and Lake Mead.

Deserts are the defining landscape of Nevada and, as such, have shaped its history, a story that involves pioneering government surveys, the construction of the first cross-country railroad, hard-rock mining (well-chronicled in Mark Twain's 1871 book *Roughing It*), nuclear testing and aircraft development, and the rise of desert boomtowns. With its natural beauty (which includes deserts, canyons, lakes, forests, and several dozen mountain ranges), extensive public land holdings (more proportionally than any other state), and action-filled casino strips in Reno and Las Vegas, Nevada is featured regularly on the big screen.

Even in the early years of cinema films were regularly made in the state, as with John Ford's 1924 silent *The Iron Horse* (see description below).

More recently, the area around Las Vegas has seen an impressive run of successful pictures, including *Oceans Eleven* (with the Rat Pack: Frank Sinatra, Dean Martin, and Sammy Davis, Jr., 1960); *Viva Las Vegas* (with Elvis, 1964); *Diamonds Are Forever* (with Sean Connery, shot partially at the Las Vegas Hilton, 1971); *The Electric Horseman* (with Jane Fonda and Robert Redford, 1979, see description below); *Starman* (with Jeff Bridges and Karen Allen, shot along the main Vegas strip, 1984); *Rocky IV* (1985, opening sequence shot at the MGM Grand); *Top Gun* (with Tom Cruise, shot on military bases near Las Vegas, as well as in southern California, 1986); *Rain Man* (with Oscar-winning Dustin Hoffman and Tom Cruise, shot partially in Caesars Palace and along the strip, 1988); *Indecent Proposal* (with Robert Redford, Demi Moore, and Woody Harrelson, shot at the Las Vegas Hilton, 1993); *Vegas Vacation* (with Chevy Chase, shot on the strip, 1994); *City Slickers II* (with Jack Palance and Billy Crystal, shot on the strip, 1994). Two Las Vegas films of the 1990s garnered Oscars: *Leaving Las Vegas* (for Nicholas Cage as best actor, 1997; see description below) and *Casino* (for Sharon Stone as best actress, 1996). Interestingly, Warren Beatty's *Bugsy* (1991), which told the story of the creation of Las Vegas by Bugsy Malone, was filmed in California.

OPPOSITE: *Golden sunlight bathes the desert and mountains near Las Vegas. Courtesy John Murray.*

Nevada is a study in contrasts, a state with vast desert areas of quiet splendor and cities known around the world for their neon lights and fast-paced life. It offers the moviemaker and the moviegoer a striking dichotomy, a landscape in which wild nature and human nature can be viewed not only as separate entities but also as interlocking parts of a larger community.

NORTHERN NEVADA

Northern Nevada is a big, dry, windswept country. It is separated from southern Nevada roughly by U.S. 6, which enters the state on the east near Baker, traverses the vast basin and range territory, and then exits Nevada near Boundary Peak (13,140 feet, the highest peak in Nevada) and Mono Lake. The northern part of Nevada is known primarily for its mining, which includes the Ruth Copper Pit near Ely (one of the largest open mining pits in the world) and the historically rich gold and silver mining area around Carson City and Virginia City (where Mark Twain spent some time in his youth). It also includes the Reno–Lake Tahoe area, a gambling and resort center that is growing almost as quickly as Las Vegas; as well as Pyramid Lake, a favorite site of filmmakers.

The Iron Horse
One of the legendary films of the silent era—John Ford's twelve-reel classic *The Iron Horse* (1924)—was shot on location in the desert near Pyramid Lake (northeast of Reno about 34 miles). A minor rail spur of the Central Pacific, rather than the busy main line, was used. Although at the earliest stage of his career, Ford, a future six-time Oscar winner, already demonstrated impressive leadership abilities as he supervised the construction of two set towns for the film, and oversaw several thousand extras, a company of U.S. Cavalry, hundreds of railroad workers and laborers, and extensive herds of buffalo, cattle, and hors-

es. It was truly an epic production, and one fitting for the defining technological achievement of the Industrial Age—the unification of the country in the joining of the Union Pacific (based in Sacramento) and Central Pacific (based in Omaha) railway lines.

The plot focused on a young man, Davy Brandon, who is searching for his father's murderer and who becomes romantically involved with Miriam Marsh (played by Madge Bellamy), the daughter of the railroad manager. Ford selected a former boxing champion and professional stuntman, George "The Chest" O'Brien, for the role of Davy Brandon, and O'Brien went on to become one of the most popular stars of the twenties and thirties. O'Brien continued to act well into his sixties, and appeared in much later Ford productions such as *Fort Apache* (1948), *She Wore a Yellow Ribbon* (1949), and *Cheyenne Autumn* (1964). Subsequent western epics such as *How the West Was Won* (1962) pale in comparison with this lengthy (almost 12,000 feet of film compared to modern films, which are about 4,500 feet in length) but brilliant masterpiece that celebrated the landscapes and history of Nevada in a unique way.

The Misfits
The Misfits tells the story of three lost people living at the margins of a desert gambling boomtown, Reno. As an essay on human loneliness and alienation, it has spawned dozens of imitations. Most are forgettable, but a few have been quite successful (*Leaving Las Vegas*, *Casino*). The screenplay for the film was written by Pulitzer prize–winning playwright Arthur Miller, Marilyn Monroe's second husband, and the picture was directed by John Huston (Oscar-winning director of *The Treasure of the Sierra Madre* and *The African Queen*). Three characters are at the center of the drama: Gay Langland, an over-the-hill cowboy (played by Clark Gable); Roslyn Taber, a world-weary divorcee (played by Marilyn Monroe); and Perce Howland, a minor rodeo performer (played by Montgomery Clift). Essential though subordinate roles were

OPPOSITE: *John Ford celebrates the unification of the country by rail in his twelve-reel epic* THE IRON HORSE *(Fox, 1924). Courtesy Photofest.*

played by Eli Wallach (as the brooding, cynical freelance pilot Guido) and Thelma Ritter (as the wisecracking Isabelle Steers, whose superficiality provides a counterpoint to Marilyn Monroe's angst).

Together this group of unlikely characters struggle to survive, both financially and psychologically, in a town whose spiritual and aesthetic emptiness mirrors their own. The plot focuses on Langland's plan to round up a herd of wild horses and sell them to a meat-packing company for dog food. The film includes some of Gable's finest acting, especially the scene in which, suffering an alcohol-induced breakdown, he collapses, sobbing, into the arms of Marilyn Monroe. Nineteen years earlier Gable had lost his wife, Carole Lombard, in a plane crash outside Los Angeles. One has the sense that the very real pain displayed in this riveting scene is but a glimpse of what the actor carried inside all those years. Similarly fine performances are provided by Montgomery Clift and Marilyn Monroe (it would be the final film for all three). In the end, the outraged Monroe prevails and Gable releases the wild horses (which are, as she successfully points out, as much victims of this world as are their human counterparts).

As in many Southwestern films the desert landscape in *The Misfits* provides a metaphor for the emptiness of the characters. The black-and-white photography of Russell Metty quietly serves to accentuate the bleakness of their world. *The Misfits* was shot in and around Reno. Many sites no longer exist, but the Mapes Casino on South Virginia Street is across the street from the former location of the casino in which Clark Gable and Marilyn Monroe gamble in the film. Also, the County Courthouse is featured early in the film. The climactic scene with the wild horses was shot near Pyramid Lake, located about 30 miles northeast of Reno on State Route 445 (the location is on the right side of the highway in the dry lake bed of Winnemucca Lake).

SOUTHERN NEVADA

Las Vegas, the economic hub of southern Nevada, is one of the largest gambling centers in the world. Its presence can be felt on the desert landscape even thirty miles away—the speeding car and truck traffic, the steady stream of commercial jets overhead, the sprawling bedroom and resort communities. Both Hoover Dam and Lake Mead are strongly linked to nearby Las Vegas, and both have changed the desert environment dramatically. Stand-up comedians and Sinatra wannabes, gaudy floorshows and over-the-hill rock bands, slot machines and blackjack tables—all are part of the fun-filled escapism that is Las Vegas. Despite the surging urban population (over one million in the metropolitan area), southern Nevada has a vast amount of wild desert. Much of it, ironically, has been protected as de facto wilderness because of its designation as a "bombing and gunnery range." Filmmakers, and their audiences, love the southern part of Nevada (primarily the city and the area around Lake Mead), and its popularity seems only to be increasing.

The Electric Horseman

The Electric Horseman (1979), like *Coogan's Bluff* (with Clint Eastwood, 1968), *Midnight Cowboy* (with Jon Voight and Dustin Hoffman, 1969) and *Urban Cowboy* (with John Travolta and Debra Winger, 1980), examines the myth of the Southwestern cowboy in both an urban and a rural landscape. Robert Redford stars as Sonny Steele, a former rodeo champion who has been slowly undone by fame and become a commercialized caricature of his former self. In the early scenes of the picture he wears a studded, ornate cowboy outfit that lights up like a Wal-Mart Christmas tree in the dark of the casino. His champion horse hasn't fared much better—Sonny suspects the animal is being drugged before performances. In a dramatic moment that is part epiphany and

OPPOSITE: *Montgomery Clift (Perce Howland), Marilyn Monroe (Roslyn Taber), and Clark Gable (Gay Langland) in John Huston's* THE MISFITS *(UA, 1961), which was Monroe and Gable's last film. Courtesy Eddie Brandt's Saturday Matinee.*

part drunken impulse, Sonny rides the horse out of the Las Vegas casino (Caesars Palace) and up the main strip in the general direction of Utah, about one hundred miles to the east.

Once there, "The Electric Horseman" finds himself pursued by a television reporter, Hallie Martin (played by Jane Fonda). Soon a guarded friendship develops between the two. They find themselves hunted by the representatives of the corporation that own both the horse and Redford (as national spokesman for their breakfast cereal). Along the way, Sonny and his horse become modern-day folk heroes. With support from the locals, they elude capture as long as possible. In the end (recalling the closing of *The Misfits*), Redford turns the horse loose to run with a herd of wild mustangs in the desert. In the last scene, Redford is seen hitchhiking beside the road, saddle in hand. Both man and beast have found the freedom without which there can be, properly speaking, no life. Country-western singer/songwriter Willie Nelson provides an excellent performance as Redford's slippery manager.

The film is a revealing look at the complex image of the contemporary cowboy. It was directed by Sydney Pollack, who had previously directed Redford in *Jeremiah Johnson* (1972) and *The Way We Were* (1973). In addition to being filmed in Las Vegas, there was also location shooting in Grafton, Utah (for more details on that location see the section on *Butch Cassidy and the Sundance Kid*, Utah chapter).

Leaving Las Vegas

While *The Misfits* spends much of its time in the Nevada countryside, *Leaving Las Vegas* (1997) is an intensely urban film, confining most of its action to downtown Las Vegas. The film follows the downward spiral of a suicidal alcoholic, Ben Sanderson (played by Nicholas Cage), who is in the terminal stage of his disease. The other key character is a beautiful young prostitute, Sera (played by Elizabeth Shue). The two meet one night on the Las Vegas strip. After a brief conversation, they retire to Cage's hotel room, which looks like something from a William Burroughs novel. One thing leads to another and the two desperate souls soon find themselves living together in Shue's apartment.

After a period of intimacy and trust, Cage betrays Shue by sleeping with another woman. This sudden, reckless act reveals both the depth and darkness of his affliction. Shue realizes Cage is hopeless and throws him out. Instead of improving matters, though, this only causes both characters to enter a new circle of the inferno. Cage's drinking becomes ominously worse and Shue is brutally assaulted by a gang of young men in a hotel room. In the end they are reunited for one brief and tender moment, just before he dies. The protagonists of Hemingway's most nihilistic novel *The Sun Also Rises* (Jake Barnes and Brett Ashley) are gleefully happy compared to the two main characters of this drama. *Leaving Las Vegas* is one of the bleakest films ever made—right in there with *Ironweed* (1987) and *Pulp Fiction* (1994)—but it also tells a necessary story and casts a very powerful light into one of the darkest corners of the human experience. Whether we like it or not, these two lives, and many like them, are part of the landscape of the Southwest, as well as a permanent part of the human condition. Movies like *Leaving Las Vegas*, with their unflinching camera lens, hold a mirror up to the cold reality of the world and remind us of the necessity of a clear vision and a compassionate heart.

This film is a guided video tour of downtown Las Vegas. It begins with an aerial view of the main strip, shot from a helicopter. Initial ground shots highlight familiar landmarks of the strip (Las Vegas Boulevard), such as the Stardust and Caesars Palace. Nicholas Cage and Elizabeth Shue see each other for the first time on the sidewalk outside the Stardust. He later propositions her in front of the Flamingo Hilton (inside casino scenes for the film were shot on location at the Gold River Casino in Laughlin, Nevada, about fifty miles south of Las Vegas). Later,

OPPOSTIE: *Robert Redford as ex-rodeo star Norman "Sonny" Steele and Jane Fonda as television reporter Alice "Hallie" Martin make an unlikely duo in Sydney Pollack's* THE ELECTRIC HORSEMAN *(Universal, 1979). Courtesy Photofest.*

Elisabeth Shue as Sera plays the modern good-hearted prostitute, a classic Western archetype, in Mike Figgis' nihilistic LEAVING LAS VEGAS *(UA, 1995). Courtesy Photofest.*

Cage and Shue go to his room at The Whole Year Inn (room #207). The scene in which Shue asks Cage to come live with her is shot outside Circus-Circus (on Las Vegas Boulevard just south of Sahara Avenue). When they leave town for a short trip they stay at the Desert Song Motel.

The film was nominated for three Oscars. Cage received what is likely to be the first of several Oscars for his unforgettable performance as Ben Sanderson.

OTHER LOCATIONS IN NEVADA

VALLEY OF FIRE STATE PARK (Drive east of Las Vegas about 45 miles on Interstate 15 and turn right or south on State Route 169; follow about fifteen miles)—Valley of Fire State Park includes some of the most striking geological formations in the lower desert near Lake Mead. The park protects an area around six miles long and four miles

Marilyn Monroe

Like so many great beauties, Marilyn Monroe seemed doomed to the saddest and loneliest of lives, never to know true love, and forever to be regarded as a trophy and an object. Born Norma Jean Mortenson in Los Angles on June 1, 1926, Marilyn Monroe grew up in difficult circumstances. Her mother, who worked occasionally as a negative cutter at Columbia and RKO, had a history of mental illness. Monroe never knew who her father was. His identity remains a mystery to this day. When Monroe was five her mother was committed to a mental institution. For the rest of her childhood Monroe lived in a succession of foster homes, each worse than the last. These traumatic experiences would scar her for life. At sixteen she dropped out of high school and married a twenty-one-year-old factory worker, a man whom by her later accounts she never cared for.

In 1944, Marilyn Monroe was discovered by a portrait photographer who asked her to pose for a pinup calendar. The calendar became a nationwide sensation and within months she was signed by Twentieth Century-Fox. Thereafter began a slow, painful climb to the top of the movie world, first in small forgettable roles, and later—as directors realized her unusual gift for comedy—in major productions. Two films in her career stand out in terms of the Southwest. The first—*Bus Stop*, 1956—was partially shot in Phoenix, Arizona. Based on the play by William Inge, *Bus Stop* was the movie in which Monroe first demonstrated her natural acting abilities. She also performed a memorable rendition of the song "That Old Black Magic." The second—*The Misfits*—was shot in and around Reno, Nevada. Based on a screenplay by her third husband, Arthur Miller, the movie explored the complex relationships between four alienated characters living in the margins of a western gambling town.

Eighteen months after *The Misfits* was released, Marilyn Monroe was found dead in a rented Hollywood bungalow, possibly of a barbiturate overdose. She was thirty-six and, according to her myriad of biographers, was despondent over President Kennedy's decision to break off their romance. At the funeral Marilyn Monroe's friend and fellow actor Lee Strasberg summed it up best: "For the entire world she became a symbol of the eternal feminine." A quarter of a century later, British songwriter Elton John would express the pathos of Monroe's life no less succinctly when he entitled his popular musical tribute to her, "Candle in the Wind." It seems certain that, so long as movies are watched, the brilliant performances of this gifted but tormented actress will always command the respect and evoke the love of her audiences.

Marilyn Monroe as Cherie is a singer in Joshua Logan's BUS STOP *(20th-Fox, 1956). Courtesy Photofest.*

wide, with weird, jagged red sandstone formations. It is a photographer's paradise and has often been used by movie directors as a filming location. This is the area in which Malcolm McDowell and Captain Kirk battled to the death in *Star Trek VI: Generations* (1994). It looks exactly like the place it was supposed to be in the film—the surface of an alien world far from the civilized precincts of the United Federation of Planets.

HOOVER DAM (Located about 30 miles southeast of Las Vegas on U.S. 93)—This distinctive structure, one of the monumental engineering feats of the Great Depression, has appeared in numerous films, most notably *Vegas Vacation* (with Chevy Chase, Randy Quaid, and Beverly D'Angelo, 1994). This is the place where Chevy Chase becomes separated from the dam tour group and winds up in a precarious position on the outside of the dam.

RENO (Located on Interstate 80 about 8 miles east of the California border)—Reno has appeared in dozens of films over the years, including *The Misfits* (see description above), *Melvin and Howard* (with Mary Steenburgen in an Oscar-winning role, 1980), *Promised Land* (with Kiefer Sutherland and Meg Ryan, 1987), and *Pink Cadillac* (with Clint Eastwood and Bernadette Peters, 1989). Nearby Pyramid Lake, Nevada's largest natural lake (not counting the man-made Lake Mead), has served as a location of films from *The Iron Horse* to *The Misfits* (see descriptions of both films above), to, more recently, *The Doctor* (with William Hurt, 1991).

CARSON CITY (The capital of Nevada, Carson City is located about 20 miles south of Reno on U.S. 395)—John Wayne's last major film *The Shootist* (with Jimmy Stewart, Lauren Bacall, and Ron Howard, 1976) was shot in and around Carson City (also at Washoe Lake State Park,

just to the north of Carson City on U.S. 395). The cattle ranch that inspired the popular television show of the 1960s, *Bonanza* (with Michael Landon and Lorne Greene), is located on State Route 28 near Carson City on the shores of Lake Tahoe (100 Ponderosa Ranch Road near Incline Village). The ranch is open for visitors from around Easter to Halloween. Other films with significant footage shot at private locations in the Carson City–Lake Tahoe area include *Misery* (with James Caan and Kathy Bates, 1990), *The Godfather, Part II* (directed by Francis Ford Coppola, 1974), *The Bodyguard* (with Kevin Costner and Whitney Houston, 1992), and *Cobb* (with Tommy Lee Jones, 1994).

SNAKE VALLEY (Located along State Route 487 between Baker, Nevada, and Garrison, Utah)—This was the area in which the classic silent film *The Covered Wagon* was shot in 1922. *The Covered Wagon* was the first real epic Western (over 9,000 feet of film) and helped to establish the career of director James Cruze (who had grown up as a Mormon in Utah and went on to become a dominant force in early cinema). *The Covered Wagon* dramatized an event that was then (in 1922) not so far distant in time—the massive historical drive to settle the western territories along the Oregon Trail. The film, with its meticulous attention to detail and strong narrative, is still studied by those planning to produce historic epics and documentary films.

OPPOSITE: THE MISFITS *(UA, 1961) and other films were shot in northern Nevada's Pyramid Lake area. Courtesy John Murray.*

ARIZONA

The first major film to be produced in Arizona was *Robber's Roost* in 1933. The studio was Twentieth Century Fox, the director David Howard. The picture featured Maureen O'Sullivan, who would later play Jane to Johnny Weismuller's Tarzan in the popular MGM jungle movies, and George "The Chest" O'Brien, whose acting would also be featured in John Ford's silent epic *The Iron Horse* (and who would years later accept a major role in John Ford's *Fort Apache*). Filming on *Robber's Roost*, which was based on a Zane Grey outlaw story, took place in Oak Creek Canyon near Sedona. In that year John Wayne was still known to his high school classmates as Marion Morrison, president of the honor society of Latin students; the Academy of Motion Pictures had not yet been created; and Warren G. Harding was president (he would die later that year and be replaced by his vice president, Calvin Coolidge). The film industry was in its infancy—still drinking from the warm bottle in the crib, so to speak—but already it was in Arizona.

Much has changed about film as an art form and as a business since then, but the landscape of Arizona continues to inspire cinematographers and to move film-viewing audiences. Arizona is a landscape that takes the heart by storm. See it once—the luminous abyss of the Grand Canyon, the bold colors of the Painted Desert, the sudden swell of the San Francisco Peaks, the haunting sentinels of Monument Valley, the quiet beauty of the Sonoran Desert—and the lifelong romance begins. It is a land, too, that resonates with strong associations from the old frontier days—the historic haunts of Cochise and Geronimo in the Dragoon Mountains, the rutted trail of the Butterfield-Overland Stage near Fort Bowie, the abandoned mines in the hills above Tombstone. Many decades will pass, and much about this world will change. Presidents and their Congresses will come and go, science will bring forth its steady stream of new inventions, this book and its author will pass unnoticed into oblivion, but one thing will remain the same—each year films will continue to be made in the enduring landscape that is Arizona, and each year audiences will flock to see them.

Monument Valley

The story of how Monument Valley became a filmmaking location begins with a visionary pioneer named Harry Goulding. Born on a ranch near Durango, Colorado, in 1897, the young Goulding first saw Monument Valley in 1923. A sheepherder by trade, he saw prospects for the little-known area and established a small trading post near the permanent spring on the north side of Oljeto Mesa. The stock market crash of 1929 and the ensuing Great Depression years were hard on the fledgling business. After surviving the long, dry years of the 1930s, the

OPPOSITE: *Rugged mountains, towering saguaro cactus stands, and colorful desert wildflowers have been attracting filmmakers to Arizona for decades. Courtesy John Murray.*

Goulding (like the rest of the country) realized that he needed to move in some new directions. Opportunity presented itself in 1939, when Goulding learned that a Hollywood studio was looking for a location to shoot a major Southwestern movie.

A few years earlier he had befriended the landscape photographer Josef Muench, who had moved to the United States to avoid persecution from the Nazis in his native Germany. Goulding called on his friend Muench and persuaded him to prepare a booklet of 8 x 10 contact prints featuring the most dramatic formations of Monument Valley, including the Mitten Buttes, the Three Sisters, and the North Window. Goulding then took these photographs to Hollywood and showed them to director John Ford. Ford was generally familiar with Monument Valley from George B. Seitz's classic silent film *The Vanishing American* (1925), which was filmed there. As soon as Ford saw the photos, he and his location manager agreed the film *(Stagecoach)* had to be shot in Monument Valley. Over the next twenty-five years John Ford would shoot nine of his most influential films in the area, and his success would attract many other directors to the Four Corners region. Eventually the area between Monument Valley and Moab, Utah, would become one of the most important filmmaking locations in the Southwest.

The novelist Willa Cather, in her novel *The Professor's House,* gave perhaps the best physical description ever of the unique landscape that is Monument Valley:

> From the flat red sea of sand rose great rock mesas, generally Gothic in outline, resembling vast cathedrals. They were not crowded together in disorder, but placed in wide spaces, long vistas between. This plain might once have been an enormous city, all the smaller quarters destroyed by time, only the public building left. . . . This mesa plain had an appearance of great antiquity, and of incompleteness; as if, with all the materials for world-making assembled, the Creator had desisted, gone away and left everything on the point of being brought together, on the eve of being arranged into mountain, plain, plateau.

Indeed, Monument Valley is a landscape that seems alternately to have come from the Book of Genesis or the imagination of Maynard Dixon.

Geologically, there is no other place on the planet quite like Monument Valley. The valley (actually, an expansive high basin) is part of what the scientists called the Monument Upwarp, an enormous plateau of Triassic and Jurassic formations that stretches from the San Juan River in southern Utah south across the red sand desert toward the region of Kayenta on the Navajo Reservation. While the softer sedimentary stones have eroded away, the more resistant rocks—Permian DeChelly Sandstone—have remained, forming high, isolated buttes, mesas, and spires. These dramatic formations tower as much as one thousand feet over the surrounding desert. Generally, the bases of the formations are made of shale, which tend to erode into stair-like rock terraces (as on the Mitten Buttes near the park visitor center). The orange-red spires and other more towering formations are made of the two-hundred-million-year-old DeChelly Sandstone.

Today, the Monument Valley area is protected as a tribal park on the Navajo Reservation. Each year more than a million people make a pilgrimage to the area. The park is reached via U.S. 163, which runs for 50 miles from Kayenta, Arizona, to Mexican Hat, Utah. The park is located just off U.S. 163 about 24 miles north of Kayenta (turn right at the entrance and drive east 4 miles to reach the visitor center). Visitors to Monument Valley should also take the road to Goulding's historic trading post (turn left at the intersection with the park entrance and drive west for 1 mile to reach Goulding's). Goulding's, which includes a restaurant, motel, and gift shop, has a fine museum, which includes many artifacts from the "Golden Age" of filmmaking. Just up the hill from the museum is the actual cabin used by Captain Nathan Brittles (John Wayne) in *She Wore a Yellow Ribbon*, with the props used in film-

John Ford

In an interview with film director Peter Bogdanovich *(The Last Picture Show)*, John Ford once observed that "I tried to copy the Frederic Remington style [in *Stagecoach* and *She Wore a Yellow Ribbon*]—you can't copy him 100 percent—but at least I tried to get in his color and movement, and I think I succeeded partly." Ford saw himself as inheriting the myths of the frontier that had been given such dramatic life in the paintings of Frederic Remington and others. Ford thought of himself not so much as portraying history as that of painting a landscape, which was also a metaphor for the American character. No one has ever received more Oscars (six) or has done a better job at creating great works of art from the raw material—deserts and mountains, clouds and sky, men and women—of the Southwest.

For this task Ford had the most unlikely of backgrounds. Born Sean Aloysius O'Feeney, Ford was the thirteenth child of first-generation Irish immigrants. His father owned a saloon in Portland, Maine, and it was here that Ford received a front-seat, Shakespearean education on life, as he observed many of the scenes that would one-day reappear in his films: tragicomic lovers' quarrels, lively back room card games, bar stool raconteurs spinning picaresque yarns,

local prostitutes and late-evening attorneys, resident bullies and anonymous heroes. After graduating from high school Ford and his brother lit out for Hollywood, where they soon found entry-level work on the film lots. Ford appeared briefly in *The Birth of a Nation* in 1915 and later began working in the directorial ranks, for which he displayed a natural ability.

His first significant film was *The Iron Horse* (1924), which was shot on location in Nevada. The production, which chronicled the Herculean effort to construct the first transcontinental railroad after the Civil War, involved thousands of extras, railroad workers, Asian laborers, and Native Americans, as well as enormous buffalo, cattle, and horse herds. It was a difficult test of Ford's leadership and organizational skills, and the thirty-one-year-old director succeeded brilliantly. The twelve-reel epic is considered one of the masterpieces of the silent era.

With the advent of sound, Ford's reputation continued to grow, as he undertook such projects as *The Lost Patrol*, *Stagecoach*, and *The Grapes of Wrath*. Many of his best films—from *Stagecoach* (1939) to *Cheyenne Autumn* (1964)—were shot in Monument Valley, which has since come to be known as "Ford Country." An entire generation of actors—

John Wayne, Henry Fonda, Maureen O'Hara, Jimmy Stewart—owed an enormous debt to this master storyteller and popularizer of the lost frontier. One can imagine an American cinema without various noted directors, but an American cinema without John Ford would be impossible to conceive.

John Ford's favorite photograph of himself shows him overlooking Ford Point in Monument Valley. Courtesy Allen Reed Collection.

ing still in place. The site of the movie-set town built for *My Darling Clementine* was about one-half mile north of the museum and trading post, out on the sage and cactus flats.

Camping is available both at Goulding's (70 sites in the canyon behind the trading post) and at the park (84 sites). Traditional Navajo hogans (eight-sided log structures) can also be rented by the night. The author of this book recommends that visitors do not drive their vehicles on the park road in Monument Valley (the road is in poor shape), but instead take one of the specially guided tours led by resident Navajos in comfortable four-wheel-drive vehicles. This helps to support the local economy on the Reservation and also saves your vehicle from what happened to Clarke Griswold's car in *National Lampoon's Vacation*.

Stagecoach

In 1938 John Ford, a forty-three-year-old film director for Twentieth Century Fox, read a short story in *Collier's* magazine entitled "Stage to Lordsburg." Ford was immediately struck by the cinematic potential of the story—a colorful group of stagecoach travelers journeying across Old Arizona during an Apache uprising—and took the idea to studio heads. They liked the proposal, and suggested Ford try to sign two top stars—Gary Cooper and Marlene Dietrich. Ford (always with an eye toward saving money and increasing profitability) had other ideas for casting. He soon hired his friend John Wayne, a hard-working B-grade actor (with sixty films in fifteen years to his credit), and Claire Trevor, a gifted young actress. Trevor, like Wayne, was destined to one day win an Academy Award (Trevor for *Key Largo*). A few months after Ford's visit with studio executives, *Stagecoach* was shot in Monument Valley on a budget of $500,000. The film, released on March 2, 1939, would eventually win two Academy Awards and gross $1.3 million in a year that saw the release of such major competitors as *Gone With the Wind*, *The Wizard of Oz*, *The Roaring Twenties*, *Mr. Smith Goes to Washington*, and *Dark Victory*.

The story line of *Stagecoach* is as old as Chaucer, as lively and earthy as anything in Shakespeare, and as contemporary as a Sam Shepard production. In the film a random assemblage of ordinary people—an alcoholic doctor (played by Thomas Mitchell, who would win an Oscar for his performance), an Army officer's pregnant wife, a traveling salesmen, a ne'er-do-well gambler, a U.S. Marshal, a prostitute with a compassionate heart (Claire Trevor), and a professional outlaw (John Wayne)—undertake a long and hazardous trip together. Along the way two of the passengers fall in love—John Wayne, playing The Ringo Kid, and Claire Trevor, playing Dallas, the "cafe dancer." Both undergo profound character changes (Wayne rejecting the independent outlaw life for a responsible role in society and Trevor allowing herself, finally, to fall in love). Seen at the distance of more than half a century, the short (ninety-seven minutes) but pithy film is an allegory of 1939 America, as the country was just then emerging from the "wilderness journey" of the Great Depression years, and was searching, in films such as this one, for a happy ending to the long national travail.

Many experts believe this film was John Ford's finest Western, if not the best Western of all time. *Stagecoach* has been called everything from "the perfect Western" to the "movie that invented the modern Western." Certainly it has become a virtual anthology of scenes, skits, and techniques that have inspired and guided generations of film directors. One of the most important aspects of the film is Ford's use of Monument Valley—its empty landscapes and dramatic monoliths—as a central, if unnamed, character in the story (indeed, as the expansive character of America itself). Ford's innovative use of "negative space"—of characters and actions starkly positioned in vast unpopulated landscapes—has been imitated, if never equaled, in dozens of lesser films.

Equally important to *Stagecoach* was the emergence of John Wayne as a film star. According to his co-star Claire Trevor, John Ford took great pains to educate John Wayne during the course of filming (Wayne was encouraged to use a more understated style emphasizing the eyes and body language more than dialogue or stock action to convey meaning). In later years she recalled that "It was tough for Duke to take [the pressure Ford put on him to act well in the film], but he took it. And he learned eight volumes about acting in that picture." In so doing Ford

A squad of cavalry serve as an escort through hostile Indian country in John Ford's STAGECOACH *(UA, 1939). Courtesy of the Academy of Motion Picture Arts and Sciences.*

John Wayne

As a child, seeking to escape a turbulent home life, Marion Michael Morrison spent hours in the local theater watching silent movies. When Rudolph Valentino's war epic *The Four Horsemen of the Apocalypse* came to town, the future Oscar-winner sat through the movie nearly a dozen times and memorized every line. After high school he attended the University of Southern California on a football scholarship and worked summers as a set-laborer on the nearby Fox film lot. It wasn't long before he was spotted by one of the young directors, John Ford, who began to feature the friendly kid called "Duke" (because of his six-foot-four-inch height and easy-going self-confidence) as a minor player in various films. Wayne would later humorously recall that "In high school I had a four-year average of 94 in all my subjects, and in college I took Latin and Romance languages and calculus, and when I started in the movies they had to teach me to say 'ain't.'"

In 1930, Wayne was given his first significant role in Raoul Walsh's Oregon Trail epic *The Big Trail* (shot in Jackson, Wyoming). Although the film did not do well commercially—a full-scale Western production was still a few years ahead of its time—*The Big Trail* did prove that John Wayne, as he was soon known, could carry his own in a major picture. His next break, after years of toiling in B-grade movies, came in the role of the Ringo Kid in John Ford's *Stagecoach* (1939), the Monument Valley Western that would eventually win two Oscars. For the next forty years, John Wayne would star in literally dozens of movies shot across the Southwest, from Monument Valley *(Fort Apache, She Wore a Yellow Ribbon, The Searchers)* to the Alabama Hills near Mount Whitney *(Blue Steel, Tycoon)*, and from south Texas *(The Alamo)* to central New Mexico *(Chisum)* to southern Colorado *(The Cowboys)*. In 1969, he was awarded an Oscar for his performance as Rooster Cogburn in *True Grit*. In 1979, he received a special life-time achievement Oscar. The last filming he did, a few months before his death from cancer in 1979, was in his beloved Alabama hills near Mount Whitney (where he had made such films as *Westward, Ho* nearly half a century earlier).

In January 1999, the annual Harris poll of America's favorite movie stars revealed that John Wayne, who had been dead for twenty years, was still holding steady in second place, behind Harrison Ford and in front of Mel Gibson. John Wayne's enduring popularity with the general viewing public continues to confirm the ardor of his fans, defy the grousing of his critics, and stand the ultimate test of time. For many, John Wayne remains the embodiment of American spirit—that riddle of an enigma of a paradox.

John Wayne as Sheriff John Chance in Howard Hawks' RIO BRAVO *(Warner Bros., 1959). Courtesy Photofest.*

transformed the thirty-two-year-old matinee actor into the disciplined, master character player the world knows today.

The Monument Valley scenes in *Stagecoach* were shot in locations that are still quite accessible today, such as in the open desert country known as Stagecoach Wash due south of Redlands Pass on U.S. 163 (Redlands Pass is eight miles southeast of Mexican Hat, Utah) and in the immediate vicinity of the Mitten Buttes, which is reached on the self-guided auto tour in Monument Valley Navajo Tribal Park. In fact, the stagecoach in the film was shot on the same dirt road that now winds through the park, as well as on the dirt access road that connects the valley with the main highway. Brief parts of the film (such as the chase scene over the Mojave salt flats and the river crossing among the live oaks) were filmed in southern California (in what is today Death Valley National Park near Furnace Creek and at the Paramount Ranch east of Malibu, respectively).

She Wore a Yellow Ribbon

She Wore a Yellow Ribbon (1949) opens with a recollection of the June 25, 1876, Custer massacre: "Custer is dead and around the bloody guidons of the Seventh Cavalry lie the two hundred and twelve officers and men he led. . . ." The narrator reports that the whole western frontier is now threatened by a massive Indian uprising. Although the historical event actually occurred in Montana and involved the northern Plains Indians, the camera pans across the desert landscape of Arizona's Monument Valley (the film would win an Academy Award for best cinematography). What director John Ford wanted was not the rolling grassy hills of the northern plains, but, rather, an idealization of the bleakness and inhospitability of the wild frontier. Monument Valley, with its stark rock formations and endless expanses of desert sand, was perfect for that. Ford shared an aesthetic point of view that had first been espoused by nineteenth-century landscape artists such as Thomas Moran, who wrote in 1879 that "I place no value upon literal transcripts from Nature. My general scope is not realistic; all my tendencies are toward idealization. . . .Topography in art is valueless."

Ford wanted colorful myth and exciting legend based in reality, but not the dull facts and dry prose of reality itself.

Later in life, John Ford, in an interview with fellow film director Peter Bogdanovich (see Texas section, *The Last Picture Show*), would admit that he had carefully studied Frederic Remington's 1907 painting *Downing the Nigh Leader*, which depicts a stagecoach being pursued by Indians on horseback, in designing the chase scene in *Stagecoach*. The chase scene in *She Wore a Yellow Ribbon* also evokes another famous Remington canvas—*Cavalry Charge on the Southern Plains*—which similarly depicts an intense moment of conflict that involved tremendous speed and violent action.

She Wore a Yellow Ribbon is a movie about the end of something. As Captain Nathan Brittles undertakes his final patrol, the audience understands that the old frontier Brittles embodies, with all its simplicities and innocence, is over. Something new, something more complex

SHE WORE A YELLOW RIBBON *(RKO, 1949) was John Ford's fourth Monument Valley film and the second in his cavalry trilogy. Courtesy Eddie Brandt's Saturday Matinee.*

that the young warriors have no means of mounting an attack) the audience knows that these Hotspurs will one day have horses again, and that there will probably be trouble anew. The film, in this sense, tells the timeless story of the battle between good and evil, the peaceful and those who disrupt the peace, those who let history change them and those who change history.

As *She Wore a Yellow Ribbon* (from the title of the old military marching song) progresses, Ford's camera moves actively around the landscape of Monument Valley. Virtually all of the formations viewed on the Navajo tour of the inner valley can be seen in the film. These include, in order of their appearance on the tour, the Mitten Buttes, Ford Point, the Sand Dunes, Totem Pole and Yei-Bi-Chei, Clye Butte, and the North Window (especially fine is the North Window, with its commanding view of the north end of Monument Valley). Those who drive back to Goulding's can visit the cabin where Captain Nathan Brittles lived directly behind the museum (it is maintained just as John Wayne left it). Although a false fort front was built at the base of the Mitten Buttes (a location seen first, to the north, on the tour), most of the inside scenes were shot at Goulding's. The shot of the Indians charging over the river was filmed on the San Juan River within sight of Mexican Hat (a distinctive rock formation) about twenty-five miles north of Monument Valley on U.S. 163.

The Searchers

It is difficult to imagine a mature male actor in Hollywood today who would have the courage or the ability to portray Ethan Edwards, the dark character played by John Wayne in John Ford's 1956 film *The Searchers*. When Wayne was awarded the Oscar in 1969, it was as much for having taken on difficult characters such as Ethan Edwards as for his having performed well in the enjoyable role of federal marshal Rooster Cogburn. *The Searchers* is Ford's most ambitious film, for it plumbs the very depths of the human soul—the darkness that lurks within us all—and in that sense it is Ford's most Shakespearean film (for Shakespeare, too, gave us characters good and bad, sometimes

John Wayne riding in front of "The Mitten" in Monument Valley creates a timeless iconography of man and monument in John Ford's SHE WORE A YELLOW RIBBON *(RKO, 1949). Courtesy Eddie Brandt's Saturday Matinee.*

and also something more sinister, is about to begin. In this sense, the film accurately reflects its time—the post-World War II period when the old adversaries (Germany and Japan) were vanquished and an even more set of dangerous adversaries—communist Russia, eastern Europe, Korea, and China—were appearing. Although Captain Brittles postpones an almost-certain war by stampeding the Indian's horses (so

Ward Bond (Reverend Captain Samuel Johnson Clayton), Jeffrey Hunter (Martin Pawley), and John Wayne (Ethan Edwards) search for a niece captured by Indians in John Ford's THE SEARCHERS *(Warner Bros., 1956). Courtesy Allen C. Reed.*

even equally good and bad, and then let us form our own judgments). Ford took a lot of risks in the film, as did Wayne, and most critics agree both director and actor succeeded brilliantly. The film also featured one of the important early screen appearances of then-sixteen-year-old Natalie Wood (a year earlier, in another precocious performance, she had been nominated for an Academy Award for her work opposite James Dean in *Rebel Without a Cause*). Most of the film is absorbed in Ethan Edwards' search for Debbie Edwards, the character played by Natalie Wood, a young woman who was captured as a child by the Comanche. The suspense is created because the audience does not know whether he will kill his niece (because, while in captivity, she has grown up and become the wife of a notorious Comanche chief and Edwards hates Indians), or let her live.

In the first scene of the film Ethan Edwards, an ex-Confederate army officer, is seen returning home to the family ranch after the Civil War. The northern buttes and spires of Monument Valley are clearly in view, the scene having been shot south of the Mitten Buttes looking north (the best long-distance shot in the area). Almost all the important camera work for the film was done within a six-mile radius of that point (except the winter scenes and the buffalo slaughter, which were shot in western Colorado). The ranch house was built just below what is today the park visitor center, so much of the early filming was done in and around that location. Later, the camera moves deeper into the valley, as when the character Brad Jorgensen (Harry Carey, Jr.), learning of his fiancée's death (Debbie's older sister, Lucy, played by Pippa Scott) runs to his own death at the Comanche encampment. In this scene Ford positioned the actors (John Wayne, Jeffrey Hunter, and Harry Carey, Jr.) on a sand dune south of the Right Mitten Butte. Still later, the scene in which John Wayne and Jeffrey Hunter visit the Indian encampment, and have words with the chief, was shot northeast of the Totem Pole and Yei-Bi-Chei. Finally, the climactic scene, in which John Wayne chases and captures Natalie Wood, was shot on the sand dunes just to the south of the Sand Spring (all of these locations are covered on the Navajo inner valley tour).

Sergeant Rutledge

If William Faulkner had grown up in Arizona instead of Mississippi, he might have written a story of racial injustice as compelling as that told in John Ford's *Sergeant Rutledge*. The film (one of the few Ford Westerns that does not include John Wayne in its cast) relates the account of a black cavalry sergeant (played by Woody Strode) who is falsely accused of raping a white woman and of murdering her father (his commanding officer). Although the film begins in a courtroom during a military court-martial, it soon moves outdoors, into the timeless landscape of Monument Valley, as each witness tells his or her story and the flashbacks begin (in the manner of Akira Kurosawa's *Rashomon*). Although the prosecuting attorney tries to implicate Sergeant Rutledge in the crimes, the chief witness, Marcy Beecher (played by Constance Towers) testifies on behalf of Sergeant Rutledge, and he is eventually acquitted (after another man confesses). The last scene shows Sergeant Rutledge riding by with his old unit, the Ninth Cavalry, as his military attorney, Lieutenant Tom Cantrell (played by Jeffrey Hunter) and Marcy Beecher look on.

Sergeant Rutledge contains some of Ford's finest camera work in Monument Valley. Perhaps the great director knew he was nearing the end of his career, and wanted to make a film that really did exceptional justice to the beauty of Navajo Country (*Cheyenne Autumn*, in 1964, would be his last of nine films in the area). Ford also wanted to produce a film that made a strong statement about an important social issue of his time, the Civil Rights movement. Viewers will recognize much of the scenery of Monument Valley in the film: Spindle Station (where the massacre takes place) is located at the base of the Mitten Buttes, the body of Chris Hubble is found in the desert just south of the North Window, and there is also a sequence shot along the San Juan River near Mexican Hat (to name just a few).

In the end, *Sergeant Rutledge* is a film about one of the worst kinds of injustice—an innocent person framed for the crimes of another. Ford's achievement was to universalize that particular experience so that anyone could empathize with Rutledge's predicament. *Sergeant*

Constance Towers (Mary Beecher), Jeffrey Hunter (Lieutenant Tom Cantrell), and Woody Strode (Sergeant Braxton Rutledge) play characters that reflect racism on the frontier and America's emerging Civil Rights Movement in John Ford's SERGEANT RUTLEDGE *(Warner Bros., 1960). Courtesy Museum of Modern Art.*

Rutledge is one of the few films made in 1960 that can still, many decades later, be watched attentively. If the local library or video store does not have it, don't worry—the film is shown on an almost weekly basis on one cable station or another.

Other Monument Valley Films

Many other films have used the landscape of Monument Valley significantly, if only partially. These include *The Ten Commandments* (with Charlton Heston as Moses wandering through the wilderness near the Mitten Buttes and also over the sand dunes west of Totem Pole and Yei-Bi-Chei), *2001: A Space Odyssey* (a lingering shot of the famous horizon), *Easy Rider* (a quick passage along U.S. 163, as well as a campsite overnight at the Mitchell Mesa cliff dwelling south of the park entrance road), *The Eiger Sanction* (Clint Eastwood rock climbing atop the pinnacles), *National Lampoon's Vacation* (Chevy Chase happily lost in the sand dunes west of Totem Pole and Yei-Bi-Chei), *Back to the Future* (a momentary visit by Michael J. Fox along U.S. 163), and *Forrest Gump* (Tom Hanks jogging on U.S. 163 just south of Redlands Pass, with the north end of Monument Valley—from Eagle Mesa to Sentinel Mesa—in view directly to the west).

Lake Powell/Page Area

Films shot in and around Lake Powell and Glen Canyon include THE GREATEST STORY EVER TOLD *(UA, 1965),* THE PLANET OF THE APES *(20th-Fox, 1968), and* SUPERMAN III *(Warner Bros., 1983). Courtesy John Murray.*

Glen Canyon National Recreation Area is one of the most popular shooting locations in the Southwest for three reasons: first, it includes some of the best red-rock landscapes on the Colorado Plateau; second, as a national recreation area, it does not have the many film permit restrictions of a national park or a BLM/Forest Service area; and, third, because of the seasonal fluctuations of Lake Powell (which is a man-made reservoir that supplies water for irrigation and hydroelectric power) film crews are free to work in the zone between low lake level and high lake level (because seasonal run-off from the Colorado River will eventually inundate and naturally clean the area). Add to this a

major gateway community, Page, which offers all the on-site services required by film production crews, as well as good shooting weather twelve months of the year, and you have an ideal filming location.

In Glen Canyon filmmakers find a diversity of shooting locations, including such unusual sites as Rainbow Bridge, Marble Canyon near Lees Ferry, Warm Creek Bay, Padre Bay, and the Bee Hive formations. Almost all filming in Glen Canyon is done south of Gregory Butte near Last Chance Bay (about twenty-five miles by water north of the Glen Canyon Dam). Glen Canyon is known for its spectacular canyons, sheer cliffs, and exceedingly colorful terrain. Although much of the landscape is unvegetated "slickrock," there are also many miles of intermittent stream beds and occasional patches of willow, cottonwood, and salt cedar. The predominant red rock—sedimentary Navajo sandstone—is similar in appearance to that found in nearby Canyon de Chelly National Monument as well as in Monument Valley Tribal Park. All in all, Glen Canyon offers a striking desert country that can, depending on studio needs, stand in for everything from the Valley of the Dead in ancient Egypt to the Wild Western frontier of the nineteenth century to the barren landscape of another planet.

Location shooting has been popular in the Glen Canyon area since the beginning of filmmaking (as in the Old Pariah site just to the west—see the Utah section), but this became even more the case after 1994, when the California Desert Protection Act closed Death Valley National Park, and many other prime locations in the southern California desert, to both filmmaking and commercial shooting (especially automobile, fashion, and music video shoots). Films done significantly within Glen Canyon include *The Greatest Story Ever Told* (1962), *Mackenna's Gold* (1969), *Planet of the Apes* (1967), *Superman III* (1982), *Indiana Jones and the Temple of Doom* (1984), and *The Flintstones* (1992). Most of the filming for these pictures was done in the area west of Lake Powell and north U.S. 89 (accessed by driving north on State Route 230 at Big Water, about fifteen miles west of Page).

More recently, in the 1990s, two major feature films were shot primarily at Glen Canyon—*Maverick* (1993) and *Broken Arrow* (1995). The first film was shot in Crosby Canyon, northwest of Page (turn right on State Route 230 from U.S. 89 about 15 miles west of Page; follow State Route 230 north for about 10 miles, then turn right on State Route 231 and follow it 4 miles to road's end, on the shores of Lake Powell). The movie was basically an updated version of the classic television show *Maverick* (1957–1960), which starred James Garner as a frontier confidence man (a role he later successfully reprised in a somewhat different form—urban private investigator—for another television program, *The Rockford Files*). Jodie Foster and Mel Gibson co-starred with James Garner in the film version of *Maverick*. Over one million dollars was

spent by Warner Brothers building an entire Western town below the high water line at the mouth of Crosby Canyon (the set was disassembled and removed after production, and the area restored to its natural appearance). Additional footage for the film was shot in the Alabama Hills near Lone Pine, California (see the Alabama Hills section in the California chapter), and in, of all places, Yosemite National Park.

Broken Arrow was a somewhat more interesting film, from the standpoint of character and theme, but was still a motion picture designed more to make a profit than to break new artistic ground or make an enduring statement. The story line focused on the relationship between the air force pilot (John Travolta) and copilot (Christian Slater) of a stealth nuclear bomber. Travolta's character, who at first seems benign but later emerges to be deeply flawed, has decided to sell two nuclear bombs to a band of criminals (in the traditional Western, Travolta's character would have been selling the latest lever-action rifles to the Apaches). While in flight over Canyonlands National Park, Travolta ejects Slater from the plane. Because of damage sustained to the cockpit during the fight between the two, the aircraft soon crashes, and the plot, now filled with obstacles, thickens. Both men are on the ground in the desert wilderness and both want the nuclear weapons, though for different reasons: one to save them and the other to sell them. Major sequences for the film were shot in Marble Canyon near Lees Ferry (featuring Christian Slater and the national park service ranger, played by Samantha Mathis), in the Bee Hive formations a half mile west of the dam and due south of U.S. 89 (one of the fights between Slater and Travolta), and along State Route 230 north of Big Water (initial sequences of Slater on the ground near his parachute).

SEDONA/FLAGSTAFF

Sedona is located amid some of the most beautiful scenery in the Southwest—scenic Oak Creek Canyon, striking Cathedral Rock, and the surrounding oak and juniper countryside studded with vermilion and sand-colored monoliths and buttes. As the introduction for this chapter pointed out, some of the first silent Western movies were shot in Sedona, film producers recognizing even then the aesthetic value of the unique landscape. Although some private ranches were used historically by the film industry (most notably, that of Bob Bradshaw), public land was also present in abundance, in the form of Coconino National Forest. As a result, many of the local rock formations are as familiar to moviegoers as the monoliths of nearby Monument Valley: Cockscomb, Chimney Rock, Capitol Butte, Sugar Loaf, Coffee Pot Rock, Mt. Wilson, Steamboat Rock, and, loveliest of all, Cathedral Rock.

Cathedral Rock—a distinctive castlelike mass of red rock pinnacles—can be found above Oak Creek in Sedona (just off Highway 179 to the west via Verde Valley School Road). This famous rock formation can be seen in dozens of movies filmed in the Sedona area, including *Blood on the Moon* (1948), with Robert Mitchum, Walter Brennan (the first actor to win three Oscars—*Come and Get It, Kentucky,* and *The Westerner*) and Barbara Bel Geddes (later Mrs. Jock Ewing on the long-running 1980s television show *Dallas*). In *Blood on the Moon* Mitchum played a gunman who switches sides to defend a rancher-woman (Barbara Bel Geddes) against the local troublemakers (a conventional theme in Westerns). Mitchum (as gunfighter Jimmy Garry) makes his campsite one night within sight of the Cathedral Rock formation. Many of the other distinctive features of Sedona country were used as background in this film. The same is true of several other B-grade films of the period, most notably *Angel and the Badman* (with John Wayne, 1946), *Broken Arrow* (with Jimmy Stewart, 1950), and *The Flaming Feather* (with Sterling Hayden, 1951), all of which can be seen regularly on cable movie channels.

Another popular site in Sedona is Bob Bradshaw's ranch (2490 W. Highway 89A), which has a Western town film set as well as a museum, cattle drives (a la *City Slickers*), horseback rides, historic wagon trips, and so forth. Many of the important Western films shot in Sedona during the period from the 1930s through the 1970s saw some location work on this ranch, including *Angel and the Badman* (the first film ever produced by John Wayne), *Stay Away Joe* (with Elvis Presley, 1968),

Broken Arrow, and *The Wild Rovers* (with William Holden, 1972). Although the elder Bradshaw is now retired, the ranch continues to be operated by his family.

Much filming has also been done in the vicinity of Flagstaff, about 30 miles north of Sedona. In 1968, for example, background footage of Dennis Hopper and Peter Fonda riding their motorcycles in *Easy Rider* was shot on scenic stretches of U.S. 89 both south and north of Flagstaff (for more on the film see *Easy Rider*—New Mexico chapter). Hopper and Fonda were also filmed stopping for gas at the Sacred Mountain filling station on U.S. 89 about seventeen miles north of Flagstaff (on the road between Sunset Crater National Monument and Wupatki National Monument). Ten years later, a considerable amount of location shooting for *Comes a Horseman* (with Jason Robards, James Caan, and Jane Fonda) was done near the San Francisco Peaks north of Flagstaff.

There are two other interesting but little known facts about film history in Flagstaff. First, several of the indoor night club scenes for the 1942 film *Casablanca*—hailed by many critics as the finest film of the twentieth century—were actually shot at the Hotel Monte Vista in downtown Flagstaff (about one block north of Route 66 on San Francisco Street). Second, the director Cecil B. DeMille (1881–1959; best known for big screen productions such as *The Ten Commandments* in 1923) came very close in 1911 to constructing a major film studio in Flagstaff.

Old Tucson

Frank Sinatra, Elizabeth Taylor, Paul Newman, Audrey Hepburn, Bing Crosby, Ingrid Bergman, John Wayne, Jimmy Stewart, Burt Lancaster, Kirk Douglas, Lee Marvin, Walter Brennan, Jack Palance, Dennis Hopper, Clint Eastwood, Robert Duvall. These Oscar-winners are just a few of the hundreds of fine actors who have worked their craft at Old Tucson, a more than sixty-year-old movie set in the mountains west of Tucson, Arizona. Watch one of the movies long enough, whether it is a light-hearted comedy like *Three Amigos!* or an old-fashioned Western like *McLintock!* and you will see the familiar town buildings

and surrounding desert country of Old Tucson, one of the finest film-
ing locations in the country. Set in the midst of a rolling valley in
Tucson Mountain Park, and within a short distance of Saguaro
National Park, the set is surrounded by miles and miles of wild
Sonoran Desert: saguaro cactus, palo verde trees, ocotillo, prickly pear,
and brittlebush.

Old Tucson is a sprawling frontier town that fills some forty acres,
complete with train station, hotel, saloon, café, harness shop, Catholic
mission, corral, blacksmith's shop, theater, schoolhouse, sweet shop,
Pony Express station, taxidermy shop, laundry, brewery, town hall,
mercantile, and so forth. The town was originally built in 1939 for the
epic motion picture *Arizona*. The film starred a twenty-one-year-old
William Holden (who would fourteen years later win an Oscar for
Stalag 17) and thirty-one-year-old Jean Arthur (who would one day star
in the Oscar-winning Western *Shane*). It told the story of a determined
pioneer woman who was trying to bring civilization to the newly settled Arizona territory.

Rather than destroy the set after production, as is usually the case,
the film company decided to maintain it permanently as a working
desert movie location. Since then over three hundred films and television shows have been filmed at Old Tucson, including *The Last Outpost*
(with Ronald Reagan, 1950); *Winchester 73* (with Jimmy Stewart, 1950);
Gunfight at the O.K. Corral (1957); *El Dorado* (with Robert Mitchum,
1965); *Hombre* (with Paul Newman, 1966); *Rio Lobo* (with John Wayne,
1970); *Joe Kidd* (1972); *The Life and Times of Judge Roy Bean* (directed by
John Huston, 1972); *I, Tom Horn* (with Steve McQueen, 1978); *Three
Amigos!* (with Chevy Chase, Martin Short, and Steve Martin, 1986); and
Tombstone (with Kurt Russell and Val Kilmer, 1994). Although few people
know it, even pop artist/filmmaker Andy Warhol once worked in Old
Tucson, producing an avant-garde film in 1968 entitled *Romeo and Juliet*.

Additionally, a number of television programs have been filmed at
the location, most notably *High Chaparral*, which ran on NBC from 1969
to 1971 and starred Leif Erickson, Cameron Mitchell, and Don Collier.

The Old Tucson site is located 12 miles west of Tucson via

*Constructed in 1939 as the set for Wesley Riggles' ARIZONA (20th-Fox, 1940), Old
Tucson has since been used for many more films including MCLINTOCK! (UA,
1963) and TOMBSTONE (Warner Bros., 1994). Courtesy John Murray.*

Speedway Boulevard or Ajo Way in Tucson Mountain Park (just follow
the signs). It is open daily when filming is not in progress, and visitors
can view staged gunfights, listen to live country-western or bluegrass
music, take horse rides out on the desert, and tour the historic set. A
side trip to the nearby Arizona-Sonora Desert Museum is *highly* recommended (2 miles north on the same road). The Old Tucson site will not
disappoint—it is really something to stand on the same ground where
directors of the caliber of John Sturges, John Huston, Sam Peckinpah,
and Howard Hawks made some of their immortal movies, and where
such historic scenes as the gunfight at the OK Corral were filmed.

Hombre

Hombre, which was filmed in 1966 at Old Tucson and also on location
near Mescal, Arizona, comes out of the same narrative line as John
Ford's 1939 *Stagecoach*. Both films follow a group of people on a stagecoach trip in the desert who must deal with unanticipated circumstances. The lead character in the film is Paul Newman, who portrays

John "Hombre" Russell, a historic figure of Arizona in the 1880s who was raised by the Apaches after a raid on his parent's homestead. After coming to town on business, he leaves on a stage. The other passengers include a corrupt Indian agent (a la *Stagecoach*), a young couple, an attractive single woman, and a suspicious stranger named Grimes (played by Richard Boone). It turns out that Grimes has planned for the stagecoach to be held up so that the corrupt Indian agent, who has stolen money from an Indian account, can be robbed. Once out in the Arizona countryside, the action turns violent, and the rest of the film follows the battle between Hombre and Grimes (between good and evil). In the end, Hombre sacrifices himself so that the other passengers can live (unlike *Stagecoach,* which opted for the happy ending). Visitors to Old Tucson will recognize the set as the town where the entire first sequence—introducing the major characters, letting them interact and create a dynamic, and establishing the atmosphere—of *Hombre* was filmed.

McLintock!

This playful film, shot in Old Tucson in 1962, shows John Wayne at his late-career best—relaxed, self-deprecating, and yet still a strong and believable heroic presence. In the picture Wayne portrays George Washington McLintock, a larger-than-life cattle rancher who steps forward as a representative for the local Indians in negotiations with an Indian agent. A secondary plot involves his ex-wife (played by one of Wayne's best friends and frequent co-actors, Maureen O'Hara) and their daughter (portrayed by a young Stephanie Powers), who is being courted by, of all people, Jerry Van Dyke, as well as by John Wayne's son, Patrick. As with most John Wayne films, the story has a happy ending—the imprisoned Indian chieftains are released by the government and John Wayne and Maureen O'Hara are reunited as a couple on his ranch. Viewers of *McLintock!* will recognize the Old Tucson set

throughout the film, but particularly in the climactic scene in which, during a Fourth-of-July celebration, John Wayne chases Maureen O'Hara up and down the streets, followed by a cheering crowd of spectators. Only John Wayne could make a film like *McLintock!*, which pays deference to the genre of the Western, and creates a serious action film, while at the same time chuckling at the genre in a good-natured way.

Other Locations in Arizona

Meteor Crater (35 miles east of Flagstaff on Interstate 40)—For many miles on Interstate 40 as you approach the Meteor Crater you will see the signs. When you finally arrive there you are certain to be impressed—the chasm is a quarter of a mile deep, nearly a mile across, and about three miles in circumference. Although the meteor struck the earth fifty thousand years ago, the impact crater it left behind is still deep enough to accommodate a large cluster of sixty-story office buildings and still have room for a half dozen NFL football stadiums. The climactic scene of the popular 1984 film *Starman* took place at the rim of Meteor Crater. The film featured Jeff Bridges (son of Lloyd Bridges) as the extraterrestrial being waiting for his interstellar ride back home and Karen Allen (who had previously starred in *Animal House* and later performed opposite Harrison Ford in *Indiana Jones and the Raiders of the Lost Ark*) as his human girlfriend. So closely does the terrain of the Meteor Crater resemble the landscape of the moon that, during the 1960s, Apollo astronauts visited the site while training for their lunar geological expeditions.

Canyon de Chelly National Monument (drive north about 90 miles on U.S. 191 from Interstate 40 to reach the visitor center near Chinle)—The final scene of *Contact*, with Jodie Foster gazing off pensively into a canyon at sunset, was shot on the south rim of Canyon de

OPPOSITE: *Martin Ritt's* HOMBRE *(20th-Fox, 1967) is a pessimistic variant of John Ford's* STAGECOACH *in which a variety of western archetypes are brought together and forced to deal with each other and their surroundings. Courtesy Photofest.*

Chelly, near the turnout above White House Ruins (mile 6.4 on the auto tour east from the visitor center). Previously, the monument had only been used for one other film of note—*Mackenna's Gold* (1969), which starred Gregory Peck, Omar Sharif, Telly Savalas, Edward G. Robinson, and Burgess Meredith.

PRESCOTT (about 100 miles north of Phoenix on Route 89)—Prescott occupies a redrock and forested country very similar in many respects to that of its close neighbor, Sedona. The town was originally founded in 1864 as the territorial capital (three years later the capital moved to Tucson and eventually Phoenix was honored with the distinction). During the late nineteenth century Prescott was as notorious as Tombstone as a gold-mining boomtown with a reputation for gunfights (by the early 1900s there were three dozen saloons in town). Because of its quaint Victorian architecture and beautiful high-desert landscape, Prescott has long been a favorite of filmmakers. As early as 1912 the Selig Polyscope Company, based in Los Angeles, was making now-forgotten films such as *The Policeman and the Baby*, *A Rough Ride with Nitroglycerine*, and *Cupid in the Cow Camp* in Prescott and in the nearby Prescott National Forest. A variety of Tom Mix films were also shot in and around Prescott, including *The Law and the Outlaw*, *Pony Express Rider*, and *Riders of the Purple Sage*. Favorite local sites included the Bar-Circle-A ranch (now the Yavapai Hills development), Granite Dells, Slaughterhouse Gulch, and the two-hundred-year-old "hanging tree."

More recently, several of the later sequences in the 1962 film *How the West Was Won* were shot in and around Prescott. The film *Billy Jack* (1971) featured Dent's Ice Cream Parlour downtown and the Courthouse plaza. Most notably, *Junior Bonner* (1972), starring Steve McQueen and Robert Preston, was shot in and around Prescott and featured, among others, the Frontier Days Rodeo, the Hassayampa Hotel, and the Palace Bar. In this film Steve McQueen played an over-the-hill rodeo champion who has returned to his hometown of Prescott, Arizona. What he discovers is that his parents are divorced, his father is being hospitalized for an injury sustained while drunk, and his little brother is in the process of subdividing the family ranch. The rest of this underrated film has McQueen playing an Arizona version of the restless nonconformist character done so well by Paul Newman a decade earlier in *Hud* (see Texas chapter). *Junior Bonner*, though, has a strikingly different conclusion, as McQueen helps his father realize an old dream, and then leaves town for the next rodeo, still defiantly competing though well past his prime. This was one of the better films that the controversial director Sam Peckinpah ever made.

In 1994 several scenes of *The Getaway* were filmed in Prescott. The 1972 Sam Peckinpah original of *The Getaway* (not filmed in Arizona) starred Steve McQueen, Ali McGraw, Ben Johnson (who would win an Oscar in 1971 for his performance as Sam the Lion in Peter Bogdanovich's *The Last Picture Show*), and Slim Pickens (best known for his role as Colonel Kong, the B-52 command pilot, in Stanley Kubrick's 1964 masterpiece *Dr. Strangelove*). The 1994 version of the film (which has much the same "outlaw-on-the-run" atmosphere of *Bonnie and Clyde*) starred Kim Basinger (who would in 1998 win an Oscar for *LA Confidential*) and her husband Alec Baldwin. Much location shooting was done in the downtown area of Prescott (the chase scenes, for example, were shot along Union Street near the county courthouse).

PHOENIX (state capital of Arizona, located at the junction of Interstate 10 and Interstate 17)—Visitors to Phoenix can take in many filmmaking locations. There are literally dozens of them, and some are quite distinguished. One of Marilyn Monroe's better pictures, the 1956 film *Bus Stop* (with a script by William Inge, who also wrote the brilliant 1955 film *Picnic*) was filmed partially in Phoenix. This is the film that first proved Monroe was an actress of great ability, particularly as

OPPOSITE: *John Wayne as George Washington McLintock overlooks his cattle in Andrew McLagen's* MCLINTOCK! *(UA, 1963). Courtesy Eddie Brandt's Saturday Matinee.*

a comedian. Her lively rendition of "That Old Black Magic" is still cherished, even by the MTV and VH1 generations. The original bus terminal was located at the corner of Central and Van Buren (much of the indoor shooting was done on a sound stage in Hollywood). In the 1976 remake of Judy Garland's 1954 film *A Star is Born* Barbra Streisand performed at Tempe-Sun Devil Stadium (Arizona State University campus). Clint Eastwood filmed part of his 1977 film *The Gauntlet* in downtown Phoenix (Superior Court Complex). In 1987 a considerable amount of filming was done in Phoenix and Scottsdale for Nicholas Cage's breakaway film *Raising Arizona*. Three years later, the Phoenix International Raceway (1313 North Second Street) was used extensively for the car racing film *Days of Thunder*, with Tom Cruise. More recently, in 1995, Phoenix was the setting of *Waiting to Exhale*, based on the Terry McMillan novel and starring Whitney Houston and Angela Bassett. In 1996 *Jerry Maguire*, which featured the acting of Tom Cruise (as the sports agent), Cuba Gooding (as the football player), and Renee Zellweger (as the hard-working single mother), was filmed throughout the Phoenix area—at Sun Devil Stadium, the Cardinals Training Center, Tempe, Lost Dutchman State Park, and Apache Junction.

APACHE JUNCTION (30 miles east of Phoenix on U.S. 60)—Of all the films made on the historic ranches and in the national forest (Tonto) around Apache Junction, none are better than Sam Peckinpah's 1970 film *Ballad of Cable Hogue*, with Jason Robards and Stella Stevens. This is the classic Western tale of the rugged individualist who builds a life for himself on the old frontier.

RED LAKE (in the desert north of Kingman, near Mount Tipton on U.S. 93)—*Mars Attacks!* may not be the best film ever to come out of Hollywood, but some of its most lively outdoor scenes were shot in the desert north of Kingman (actors of the caliber of Jack Nicholson, Glenn Close, Annette Bening, and Pierce Brosnan lent their skills to this playful satire on the genre).

SUPERIOR (located near the junction of U.S. 60 and Arizona 117)—In 1996 Oliver Stone shot much of his film *U-Turn*, which featured performances by Nick Nolte, Sean Penn, and Jennifer Lopez, in and around this small (3,452 souls) town, which is located on U.S. 60 east of the dude-ranching capital of Apache Junction and west of the old mining enclave of Globe (or "Glob" as Edward Abbey called it).

TUCSON (located at the Junction of Interstate 10 and Interstate 19 in southern Arizona)—Tucson and its environs (especially Old Tucson) have long been used in film. One of the most successful recent productions was the 1995 Warner Brothers film *Tin Cup*, which starred Kevin Costner, Don Johnson, and Rene Russo in a love triangle involving two professional golfers and a clinical psychologist. The film (which was represented in the script as being in west Texas) also saw location shooting in the nearby communities of Tubac and Sonoita. The college comedy *Revenge of the Nerds*, which took up where *Animal House* left off, was filmed on the University of Arizona campus in 1984. *Lilies of the Field* (1963), with Sidney Poitier and Lilia Skala, was also filmed in Tucson. Some television shooting was originally done in this area, most notably an early episode of the *Rawhide* series in 1956, with an unknown actor named Clint Eastwood and, later, in the sixties, several episodes of such popular programs as *Route 66* and *The Fugitive*.

ELGIN (about 30 miles northeast of Nogales on State Route 82)—Howard Hawks did some filming in this area in 1948 for his movie *Red River*, which starred John Wayne, Montgomery Clift, and Walter Brennan. Filming was also done on the lower Verde River near Phoenix. However, the 1954 musical *Oklahoma!*, which was partially filmed in the nearby San Rafael Valley (the original ranch recently sold to the Nature Conservancy) and Nogales, was the area's most important film.

COCHISE STRONGHOLD (about 20 miles south of Interstate 10 on U.S. 191)—Located in the Coronado National Forest, this was the actu-

Stella Stevens as Hildy and Jason Robards as Cable Hogue lament the passing of the Old West in Sam Peckinpah's THE BALLAD OF CABLE HOGUE *(Warner Bros., 1970). Courtesy Photofest.*

al location in which the Apache chieftain Cochise maintained his head-quarters during the 1860s and 1870s. The area is known for its beautiful rock formations and desert scenery. It has been used for filming throughout the century. Most recently, it was a primary site for filming in Danny Glover's TNT movie *Buffalo Soldiers* (1997).

GREEN VALLEY (20 miles south of Tucson on Interstate 19)—Parts of Kevin Costner's megadisaster film *The Postman* (1996) as well as *Star Trek: First Contact* were filmed in Green Valley, which has been used by filmmakers since the beginning. *Star Trek: First Contact* was also filmed at the Titan Missile Base, which is located in the Green Valley area.

TOMBSTONE (on State Route 80, 24 miles south of Benson and Interstate 10)—Tombstone is a place with some history. It was here that one of the most chronicled events in the old Southwest occurred— the October 26, 1881, Wyatt Earp–Clanton Gang gun battle at the OK Corral (there is even an old *Star Trek* episode from the 1960s, with William Shatner and Leonard Nimoy, that dramatizes this piece of history). Many of the historic buildings that date to this period, including Boot Hill Graveyard (at the northern city limits) and the OK Corral (between 3rd and 4th streets on Allen street), can still be found exactly where they were more than one hundred years ago. Dozens of films have been shot on location, either wholly or partially, in and around Tombstone, including *McLintock!* (1963) and *Tombstone* (1994).

YUMA (on Interstate 8 about 170 miles west of Casa Grande)—Yuma is considered the filmmaking gateway for the Algodones Dune fields, which are actually located in the extreme southeastern corner of California (see California chapter). Actors of the stature of Rudolph Valentino *(Son of the Sheik)*, Marlene Dietrich *(Morocco, The Garden of Allah)*, Tyrone Power *(Suez)*, Gary Cooper *(Beau Geste)*, and Cary Grant *(Gunga Din)* performed on these great dunes of the lower Colorado River valley in the early 1920s and 1930s. Humphrey Bogart came here in 1943 to film *Sahara* (co-starring with a very young Lloyd Bridges). So did Harrison Ford in 1982 to film *Return of the Jedi*. In 1994 Kurt Russell filmed the science fiction adventure *Stargate*. The old territorial prison in Yuma has also been used periodically for films as well, including Sylvester Stallone's 1988 film *Rambo III*.

MUSEUMS AND MONUMENTS

REX ALLEN ARIZONA COWBOY MUSEUM (150 North Railroad Avenue, Willcox)—The Rex Allen Museum, which is located in a turn-of-the-century saloon, is a must see for classic Western aficionados as

Gordon MacRae as Curly and Charlotte Greenwood as Aunt Eller share a lighthearted moment in Fred Zinneman's OKLAHOMA! *(20th-Fox, 1955). Courtesy Eddie Brandt's Saturday Matinee.*

well as those interested in southern Arizona's colorful history and cowboy culture ($2 single, $3 couple, $5 family). Also, check out Rex Allen Days the first weekend in October.

TOM MIX MONUMENT (17 miles south of Florence on Arizona 79)— A roadside monument, topped by a riderless horse, marks the spot where movie star Tom Mix rolled his car and died on October 12, 1940.

OPPOSITE: *The sand dunes of the lower Colorado River and other Southwestern locations served as the backdrop for nineteenth-century India in George Stevens'* GUNGA DIN *(RKO, 1939). Courtesy Eddie Brandt's Saturday Matinee.*

UTAH

If you have ever watched *Jeremiah Johnson, Butch Cassidy and the Sundance Kid, Thelma and Louise,* or *The Greatest Story Ever Told,* you have seen the unique province of the Southwest that is Utah. It is a country like no other, with vast areas of high desert (including the Great Basin Desert, the Painted Desert, and the Mojave Desert), deep river canyons (the Green, San Juan, and Colorado), major lakes (Great Salt Lake, Utah Lake, and Lake Powell), and extensive mountains (the Wasatch Range, the La Sal Mountains, and the Abajo Mountains). Despite its location in the heart of the intermountain region, Utah was one of the last western states to be explored or mapped. In fact, the Henry Mountains were the last named mountain range in the country, and the Colorado River was the last river to be run in the continental United States (John Wesley Powell Expedition, 1869). Even today, there are still remote regions in the wild Utah canyon country that have not been explored on foot.

Filmmakers have been operating in Utah since the silent era. As early as 1925 director John Ford traveled to Promontory, Utah, to film part of his twelve-reel epic film *The Iron Horse,* shooting at the very place where the historic golden spike was driven, connecting the East Coast with the West Coast for the first time by rail line (which, in a larger sense, signaled the birth of modern America). During the 1930s the area around Kanab in southwestern Utah became known as "Little Hollywood" for the many pictures made there. Later, in the 1950s, the center of gravity shifted to the east, as Moab became the state's major center for filmmaking. Virtually every American director and actor of note has worked in Utah, from Cecil B. DeMille (*Union Pacific,* 1939) to John Ford (*Rio Grande,* 1950) to Steven Spielberg (*Indiana Jones and the Last Crusade,* 1989); from Henry Fonda (*My Darling Clementine,* 1946) to Clint Eastwood (*The Outlaw Josey Wales,* 1976) to Jodie Foster (*One Little Indian,* 1973). If a film has red slickrock and prickly pear cactus desert, cloudless blue skies, and distant mountain ranges, there's a good chance it was shot in Utah.

MOAB AREA

The story of how Moab became one of the most popular filming locations in the Southwest begins, not surprisingly, with the acclaimed film director John Ford. A detailed account of this essential chapter of Southwestern film history is presented in Bette Stanton's regional history *Where God Put the West, Movie Making in the Desert* (1994).*

*Anyone interested in the subject of filmmaking in southeastern Utah should read Bette L. Stanton's wonderful book *Where God Put the West, Movie Making in the Desert,* which is sold for $19.95 by the Moab to Monument Valley Film Commission, 50 East Center #1, Moab, Utah 84532, 801-259-6388.

OPPOSITE: *Located near Moab, Professor Valley was used for many films including* CHEYENNE AUTUMN *(Warner Bros., 1964). Courtesy John Murray.*

According to Stanton, who was for many decades a leader of the Moab Film Commission, John Ford had by 1949 completed four successful films in Monument Valley—*Stagecoach* (1939), *My Darling Clementine* (1946), *Fort Apache* (1948), and *She Wore a Yellow Ribbon* (1949)—and had decided to find a desert location with a slightly different look. For his next project, *Wagonmaster,* which would dramatize the struggles of the early pioneering Mormons, Ford traveled north on U.S. 191 into

Max Von Sydow portrays Jesus Christ in George Stevens' historical drama THE GREATEST STORY EVER TOLD *(UA, 1965). Courtesy Eddie Brandt's Saturday Matinee.*

southeastern Utah. Once in Moab, he was introduced by the editor of the Moab *Times-Independent* to local cattle rancher George White (who later founded the Moab Film Commission). George White drove the film director up State Route 128 to Professor Valley and the region of the Fisher Towers on the Colorado River, two of the loveliest spots in the Southwest. The redrock country around Fisher Towers is every bit as beautiful as Monument Valley, but with one added advantage— there is a large river running through it. Ford instantly realized, as he had in 1939 when Harry Goulding had shown him photographs of Monument Valley, that he had found another perfect filming location.

Since then over fifty major feature films have been made within a two-hour driving radius of Moab. Everything from action adventure films (*Indiana Jones and the Temple of Doom,* with Harrison Ford in 1989) to human dramas (*Thelma and Louise,* with Geena Davis, Susan Sarandon, and Brad Pitt in 1991) to traditional westerns (*Geronimo,* with Gene Hackman and Robert Duvall in 1993) have used the Moab area as a primary filming location. Directors can find every sort of landscape in the area, from towering spruce and aspen-covered mountains (the 12,000-foot La Sal Range), to wind-swept sand dune fields (Behind the Rocks), to dramatic mile-deep canyons (Island in the Sky), to colorful slickrock (Sevenmile Canyon), to open desert and high prairie (Green River country). The town, which has hosted filmmakers and commercial producers now for over half a century, also has a well-developed support system—lodging, restaurants, supplies, crew and production services—for location shoots.

Generally, film producers work in one of eight public and private areas in Moab. Those areas that involve public land (Arches National Park, Canyonlands National Park, Manti–La Sal National Forest, BLM) require a permit, as in other parts of the Southwest. Permits detail the impacts of filming on habitat and archaeological sites, and also insure the safety of any explosives or pyrotechnics. They also detail restoration efforts, if any, that will be necessary following the construction of sets, use of livestock, and so forth. Film production companies are charged by the government for their activities on public land, and these fees can range into many hundreds of dollars per day (there is currently a movement in Congress to increase these fees to approximate those that companies pay for filming in private areas, but the move seems fated, like those to increase grazing fees or mining fees, never to pass).

The public areas in the Moab area include the following:

ARCHES NATIONAL PARK AND CANYONLANDS NATIONAL PARK Because of national park restrictions (film crews must remain on or near paved roads), these two sites are used primarily for commercial shoots—music videos, automobile and fashion advertisements. Automobile advertisements, in particular, often feature a drive through scenic Courthouse Wash and along Park Avenue in Arches National Park (at about mile 5 on the main park road). Despite these restrictions, two major films in recent memory have seen some significant shooting in Arches. Steven Spielberg shot part of the opening sequences of *Indiana Jones and the Temple of Doom* at Double Arch (in the Windows section of Arches National Park). The scene in which Curly appears to Billy Crystal in *City Slickers II* was also shot in the Windows section of Arches National Park. Another film that saw some action in Canyonlands was *Thelma and Louise* (see movie description below). Historically, the parks were used more often, as in the "Sermon on the Mount" scene in *The Greatest Story Ever Told*, which was shot at the Green River Overlook in Canyonlands National Park (the Green River Overlook is located just off State Route 313 about 29 miles south of the intersection with U.S. 191; the general area is known as the Island in the Sky district of Canyonlands National Park).

PROFESSOR VALLEY AND FISHER TOWERS This area near Moab represents one of the most distinctive landscapes in the Southwest, especially Fisher Towers, a unique sedimentary formation that has appeared, literally, in hundreds of pieces of commercial advertising, as well as in over a dozen major films. The desert valley, with its towering redrock formations, is found along State Route 128 roughly

Double Arch in Arches National Park was used in the opening scene of INDIANA JONES AND THE LAST CRUSADE *(Paramount, 1989). Courtesy John Murray.*

between the confluence with the Dolores River (30 miles east of the intersection with U.S. 191) and the bridge over Castle Creek (16 miles east of the intersection with U.S. 191). Ninety-five percent of the land in Professor Valley is in the public domain (BLM and state land at lower elevations, Manti–La Sal National Forest at higher elevations, Arches National Park north of the Colorado River). Popular filming locations include the George White Ranch (about 14 miles east of the intersection of State Route 128 and U.S. 191 near the confluence of Castle Creek and the Colorado River), Ida Gulch (about 17 miles east of the intersection of State Route 128 and U.S. 191), the Onion Creek area (about 21 miles east of the intersection of State Route 128 and U.S. 191), and the Fisher Towers area (about 22 miles east of the intersection of State Route 128 and U.S. 191). Distinctive geological features in this extensive valley area include Castle Rock, Parrot Mesa, The Porcupine Rim, Adobe Mesa, Fisher Mesa, Priest and Nuns, Totem Pole, Titan Towers, and the Fisher Towers. Although the names may

INDIANA JONES AND THE LAST CRUSADE *(Paramount, 1989) and* BREAKDOWN *(Paramount, 1997) were partially filmed in Sevenmile Canyon near Moab. Courtesy John Murray.*

not be familiar, the features will be instantly recognizable the first time you drive through the valley (if you've ever been to the movies).

Among the many films made in Professor Valley, several stand out, including *Cheyenne Autumn* (1964), John Ford's last Western and his final apology to the Indians; *Taza, Son of Cochise* (1953), with Rock Hudson (of all people) as Taza; and *Fade In* (1967), an interesting film that actually made Moab the subject of the story. In *Fade In* Burt Reynolds (Oscar nomination, *Deliverance*, 1972) played a Moab rancher who falls in love with a member of a film production company that is in town making a picture entitled *Blue* (that film, made concurrently in Professor Valley, starred Ricardo Montalban and Karl Malden). More recently, Professor Valley served as a primary shooting location for *Geronimo* (1993—see film description below). Other major films

made in the area include *Wagonmaster* (1949—see film description below), *Rio Grande* (1950—see film description below), *Battle at Apache Pass* (1952), *Siege at Red River* (1954), *Ten Who Dared* (1959), *The Comancheros* (1961), and *City Slickers II* (1993).

SEVENMILE CANYON As its name indicates, Sevenmile Canyon is located roughly 7 miles north of Moab (drive north of Moab on U.S. 191 for about 7 miles and turn west on State Route 313, which follows Sevenmile Canyon for the next 5 miles). Although the area has seen a lot of filming action, it is probably best known for a sequence in Steven Spielberg's 1988 film *Indiana Jones and the Last Crusade* (with Harrison Ford and Sean Connery, as well as River Phoenix portraying the young Indiana). State Route 313 was also a location for the film *Breakdown*

(1996, with Kurt Russell, Kathleen Quinlan, and J. T. Walsh). That film, which tells the story of a young couple whose vehicle breaks down in the desert, also shot highway footage along U.S. 191 and State Route 128 (segments of the film were also shot in the Mojave Desert near Las Vegas).

BEHIND THE ROCKS DUNES Of the various dunefields around Moab, this is one of the most popular for filming, with an extensive basin of windswept, coral-colored dunes (reached by a well-marked but primitive access road to the west about 15 miles south of Moab on U.S. 191—this road is recommended for four-wheel-drive only).

POTASH TRAIL AND SCHAEFER TRAIL At the end of State Route 279 (the road begins off U.S. 191 2 miles north of Moab) there is a scenic road along the Colorado River that leads to the Moab Salt and Potash Mine and Mill. The area has a very unique appearance and has been often used in science fiction films, such as *Rocket Man* (1996) and *Species 2* (1997). The Schaefer Trail, a primitive dirt road, begins at the end of State Route 279 (the road is in the vicinity of Thelma and Louise Point, where the two characters in the film drove their automobile off a cliff).

Although private land is scarce in Grand County and San Juan County, about a dozen ranches around Moab have been used historically in filmmaking. One of the most popular has been the George White Ranch (offering around 700 acres and 380 head of cattle on State Route 128 about 14 miles east of the junction with U.S. 191; also 5 miles south on the Spanish Valley Road). The White Ranch was used as early as 1950 by John Ford for *Rio Grande*. More recently, the ranch was used in 1993 as a filming location in the retelling of the Geronimo story with Gene Hackman and Robert Duvall. Further south, the Pack Creek Ranch (located at the end of the Spanish Valley Road about 15 miles southeast of Moab, offering 300 acres and around 20 horses) has also seen some shooting. The Dugout Ranch—located about mile 15 on State Route 211 (the road to the Needles District of Canyonlands National Park), offering 2,000 acres and around 700 head of cattle— has been used for filming *City Slickers II* and other films. Recently, the Nature Conservancy entered into a land preservation agreement with the longtime owners of the Dugout Ranch, a site which is prized both for its scenic redrock and valley location and for its natural wetlands (always scarce in a desert region).

Wagonmaster

Wagonmaster (1949) was the first major Hollywood production to deal with the mainly Utah subject of Mormon history. Ford's task as a director and as a storyteller (Ford actually wrote this story) was to universalize the Mormons' particular experience so that people not of their faith (or even of their country) could relate to their wilderness travails. Mormons began arriving in Utah during the 1840s and 1850s, taking a cut-off from the Oregon Trail in southwestern Wyoming (old-time trapper Jim Bridger, seeking to profit from this newest wave of emigrants, established a trading post along the route). The Mormons then passed through a rugged desert and mountain country, often menaced by outlaws and other hostile elements, before settling in a long band that stretched from Logan on the north to St. George on the south. *Wagonmaster* sets itself in this early period, before the Utah territory was settled and law and order established.

The film starred several gifted young actors of the time, most notably Ben Johnson and Harry Carey, Jr., as well as Ward Bond (as the elder wagonmaster). The narrative focuses on two young cowhands (Johnson and Carey) who elect to join the caravan, and who eventually help to save it from the evil Clegg gang, among others. Much of the picture was shot in Professor Valley along the Colorado River and in Spanish Valley just southeast of Moab (some additional shooting was done in Monument Valley). One of the most beautiful scenes in this richly filmed production—the segment in which Ben Johnson and Ward Bond look for a safe river crossing—is just upriver of the Fisher Towers, along what is today State Route 128 (about 25 miles northeast of the junction with U.S. 191). In the end, *Wagonmaster* became one of Ford's most successful creations. The film presents, in the Mormons' historic pilgrimage, a metaphor for the longer journey of human life.

Harry Carey Jr. (Sandy Owens), Ben Johnson (Travis Blue), and Ward Bond (Elder Wiggs) co-star in a picture about a Mormon wagon train's struggle to reach the promised land in John Ford's WAGONMASTER *(Republic, 1950). Courtesy Eddie Brandt's Saturday Matinee.*

Both are filled with obstacles, both move from the familiar country of the past into the new and often strange landscape of the future, and both are grounded in family, friendship, and community.

Rio Grande

Rio Grande (1950) was the final installment in director John Ford's much-celebrated "Cavalry Trilogy" (the others were *Fort Apache* in 1948 and *She Wore a Yellow Ribbon* in 1949). The concept of repeating a successful paradigm is certainly nothing new to drama—one need look no further than Shakespeare, who wrote *Henry IV Part I* and then soon followed it, because his audiences loved the hilarious character of Falstaff so much, with *Henry IV Part II*. What is unique about Ford's approach to the process is that, while using the same main character (John Wayne as Lieutenant Colonel Yorke) he made each film in the trilogy very different in terms of theme. Such is the case with *Rio Grande*, which deals with a man's torn allegiances to family and to country. In the film John Wayne, as Lieutenant Colonel Kirby Yorke, finds himself serving in the same cavalry unit as his son, Trooper Jeff Yorke (played by Claude Jarman, Jr.) on a dangerous patrol across the Rio Grande in Old Mexico. Maureen O'Hara, as Colonel Yorke's wife, does her usual impeccable job as the strong frontier woman who is not reluctant to stand up to Wayne (in this case, on issues concerning the safety of their only child, Trooper Yorke). A superb performance was also provided in the film by future–Oscar winner Ben Johnson (*The Last Picture Show*, 1971—see Texas chapter) as Trooper Tyree.

Although several parts of *Rio Grande* were shot in Monument Valley, most of the filming was done in Professor Valley north of Moab. The fort, which serves as the geographic and narrative center of the picture, was built on George White's ranch in Professor Valley (south of State Route 128 about 15 miles east of the junction of U.S. 191 and State Route 128). Additional important scenes, including the various Indian attacks, were filmed in Professor Valley at the same location, in Ida Gulch (about 1 mile east of the junction of Castle Valley Road and

A stunt from one of the battle sequences in John Ford's RIO GRANDE *(Republic, 1950). Courtesy Eddie Brandt's Saturday Matinee.*

State Route 128), and at Onion Creek (about 4 miles east of the junction of Castle Valley Road and State Route 128).

Thelma and Louise

In its sympathetic treatment of the beleaguered outlaw, *Thelma and Louise* falls into a long tradition in Southwestern cinema, as seen in such films as *Stagecoach* (with John Wayne playing the likable Ringo Kid), *Blood on the Moon* (with gunfighter Robert Mitchum switching allegiances to help a woman rancher), *Bonnie and Clyde* (with everyone cheering for the good-natured Warren Beatty and Faye Dunaway), *Butch Cassidy and the Sundance Kid* (the most popular outlaws ever to roam the Wild West), and *The Getaway* (the more recent version with Kim Basinger and Alec Baldwin). The difference between *Thelma and Louise* and these other pictures is that the object of the outlaw's enmity

Susan Sarandon as Louise Sawyer and Geene Davis as Thelma Dickinson are two best friends on a four-day race against time after a weekend getaway goes awry in Ridley Scott's THELMA AND LOUISE *(MGM, 1991). Courtesy Photofest.*

in *Thelma and Louise* is not a faceless institution (like a bank), or an equally remote symbol of wealth (like the railroad magnate E. R. Harriman in *Butch Cassidy*), but, rather, the opposite gender. *Thelma and Louise* is a film about two alienated characters who find themselves in a desperate situation, and who become increasingly violent and unpredictable. The narrative culminates with their suicides. The film includes one of the first significant screen appearances of Brad Pitt,

who would go on to perform in several other successful films during the 1990s, including the Oscar-winning *Legends of the Fall* (1994).

Thelma and Louise was shot almost entirely in and around Moab, including the ghost town of Cisco (take exit 212 on I-70 and drive west 5 miles), Thompson Springs (take exit 190 on I-70 and drive west 6 miles), La Sal (9 miles east of U.S. 191 on State Route 46), Arches National Park (some of the night-driving footage was shot on the park road in the vicinity of Courthouse Wash and Park Avenue), and along U.S. 191 north and south of Moab. The climactic scene, in which the two women drive their automobile off a cliff in the Grand Canyon rather than surrender to the FBI, was actually shot on a rim below Dead Horse Point on the Potash Trail (follow State Route 279 west of U.S. 191 for 15 miles). One of the crash dummies used in this scene can be seen at the offices of the Moab to Monument Valley Film Commission in Moab (50 East Center #1).

Geronimo

The life and times of Geronimo have been represented many times in film. The Chiricahua Apache leader is one of the few historical figures of the old Southwest whose name draws a nod of recognition across the world, from Paris to Peking. Born around 1840 near the headwaters of the Gila River in New Mexico (in what is today the Gila Wilderness), Geronimo was a peaceful medicine man until his wife and children were killed in a massacre in Mexico. For many decades after (not unlike the wronged protagonists of *High Plains Drifter* or *The Outlaw Josey Wales*) Geronimo waged a relentless war against all who violated his homeland, the sprawling borderland region historians now refer to as Apacheria. After years on and off the reservations, he finally surrendered in 1886 and spent the rest of his life under military supervision in Florida and Oklahoma. Shortly before his death, in one of the ironies of history, Geronimo rode a horse in the inaugural parade of Theodore Roosevelt (who steadfastly refused to release him to go home to the Southwest, though probably more out of concern for Geronimo's safety than anything else). Geronimo's autobiography, dictated to a journalist before his death—*Geronimo, His Own Story,* edited by S. Barret (1905)—is highly recommended.

The 1993 remake of this story focuses on the campaign to subdue Geronimo during the 1885–1886 period (John Bourke's 1891 book *On the Border with Crook,* a related account, is also an excellent read). The picture featured two major stars, both Oscar-winners: Robert Duvall (for *Tender Mercies;* see Texas chapter) and Gene Hackman (for *The French Connection,* 1971). While the film (like all non-documentary films based on history) works loosely and at times imaginatively with the facts, *Geronimo* is in the end a fairly realistic picture, with particularly strong performances by both Duvall and Hackman. Much of the filming for the picture was shot in Professor Valley, including the Onion Creek area. Additional location shooting was done at the Needles Overlook (about 40 miles south of Moab on U.S. 191, turn west on State Route 211 and drive 24 miles west to the end of the road), on the Potash Trail, and on the sand dunes in the Behind the Rocks area. This picture made fine use of the Professor Valley landscapes, with some of the best local shooting since the days of John Ford.

MEXICAN HAT AND THE VALLEY OF THE GODS

Whenever John Ford was in Monument Valley and needed to film Indians crossing a river in a massed attack (as in *She Wore a Yellow Ribbon*), he drove the crew in convoy fashion up U.S. 163 twenty-five miles to Mexican Hat, Utah. Upstream of the small town there are long open stretches of flood plain, cottonwood stands, and sandy beach along the San Juan River. In 1998, this river area between Bluff and Mexican Hat gained national attention as three anti-government survivalists hid out in the area, eluding FBI agents, Navajo trackers, and local police officers (one committed suicide, two are still at large). Novelist Tony Hillerman is said to be writing a novelized version of the incident, which involved the killing of a police officer and may ultimately result in yet another Southwest outlaw film, although with a dark, modern twist.

Valley of the Gods, a somewhat similar but scaled-down version of Monument Valley, is located just north of Mexican Hat (it can be accessed from either U.S. 163, 5 miles north of Mexican Hat, or from State Route 261, 7 miles north of Mexican Hat). This area of pinnacles and buttes has been used more recently than in the past, perhaps in part because it is located on a fairly obscure parcel of public land and

Zane Grey

Few writers have seen so many works adapted into film, or had such a powerful influence on the genre as Zane Grey. Though forgotten by most, such pioneering Western films as *Heritage of the Desert* and *Riders of the Purple Sage*—both based on popular Grey novels—went a long way toward establishing the Western as a distinct cinematic form, and to paving the way—in terms of setting, theme and character—for such later classics as *Stagecoach* and *High Plains Drifter*.

Grey had the most unlikely of beginnings, considering the ultimate trajectory of his life. Born in 1872 in Zanesville, Ohio, he went on to become, of all things, a dentist. Like many working professionals, Grey secretly dreamed of becoming a successful novelist. Unlike most, though, he actually acted on his ambitions and began seriously cultivating his talent. After self-publishing his first novel (a disaster entitled *Betty Zane*), Grey traveled to Arizona at the urging of his wife, who at that time was his sole fan and cheerleader. After returning to the east, Grey holed up in a cottage and wrote *The Heritage of the Desert* (1910), which remains one of his finest books. Two years later *Riders of the Purple Sage*, another classic, appeared.

Many of the early silent films based on Grey's novels were shot on location at Old Pariah, west of Page, Arizona, on land currently managed by the Bureau of Land Management. Others were shot in the hills around Los Angeles, particularly in what is now the Santa Monica National Recreation Area near Malibu. Paramount's first sound Western, which came out in 1930, was based on Zane Grey's novel *By the Light of the Western Stars*. Starring Richard Arlen, best known for his performance in *The Virginian* (1929), as well as the lovely Mary Brian, *The Light of the Western Stars* was produced by Harry Sherman, who would later create the enormously successful Hopalong Cassidy (William Boyd) series with Paramount. Zane Grey died in 1939, the same year John Ford's *Stagecoach* appeared, and with it a whole new form of the Western Grey had helped create.

Zane Grey just after returning from a two year fishing trip in Australia and the publishing of THE LOST WAGON TRAIN. *Courtesy Photofest.*

film permitting is easier than on the heavily visited tribal lands of Monument Valley to the south. Valley of the Gods can be seen in *Forrest Gump* (1993) and in *To Wong Foo* (1994, with Patrick Swayze and Wesley Snipes).

OLD PARIAH

Old Pariah is one of the secret treasures of the Southwest. Anywhere else in the country, it would be a national park. Here it is just another sonorous place-name on a sprawling Bureau of Land Management map, visited perhaps by a few thousand people a year. With its quiet nestled valley, peaceful desert river, and nearby hills colored in rainbow bands of purple, orange, yellow, red, and blue clay, the old ghost town has found itself used as a film set since the beginning. During the 1920s, Zane Grey's stories were transformed at Old Pariah into such now-forgotten silent films as *Heritage of the Desert*. Later, major productions were set, either partially or wholly, at Old Pariah, including *Western Union* (1941, with Randolph Scott, Robert Young, and John Carradine), *The Greatest Story Ever Told* (1965), *Mackenna's Gold* (1969, with Gregory Peck, Omar Sharif, Edward G. Robinson, and Eli Wallach), and, most notably, *The Outlaw Josey Wales* (1976, see film description below).

The original townsite was established in 1870 by Mormon pioneers. In its early days, it was visited by such notables as John Wesley Powell (the explorer who first rafted down the Colorado River through the Grand Canyon). Severe flooding eventually forced the farmers out. A small gold mine operated in the area around 1911, but it too was eventually abandoned. The Old Pariah Movie Set is now maintained by the BLM as a historic site, and is often visited by elderhostel groups and other tour groups from Kanab and Page. To reach the area, drive east of Kanab for 30 miles on U.S. 89 and turn north on the dirt BLM road. Drive north approximately 4 miles and park on the south side of the river. The ghost town is within sight to the north. The dirt access road to Old Pariah is impassable to non–four-wheel-drive vehicles after rain or snow.

The Outlaw Josey Wales

The Outlaw Josey Wales (1976) is about a theme as old as the Bible: revenge ("a dish," according to the traditional Sicilian proverb often quoted by novelist/screenwriter Jim Harrison, "that is best served up cold"). In this sense, *The Outlaw Josey Wales* takes up where Eastwood's earlier (1972) *High Plains Drifter* (another vengeance narrative) left off. Whereas in *High Plains Drifter* Eastwood played a living ghost, a reconstituted spirit that has come back to visit destruction upon his tormentors, Eastwood portrayed a very human character in *Josey Wales*. This Ambrose Bierce–like story begins during the Civil War, when Wales' wife and son are killed by Union troops. Wales subsequently becomes a Confederate guerrilla raider so that he can better track down the Union officer who was responsible for the crime. At the end of the Civil War he refuses to surrender his obsessive quest, and the twilight struggle for justice continues for years, as Wales finds himself fighting various troops, Indians, and outlaws. In the end, Eastwood, having let his fury run its natural course, returns to his old farming life.

Much of the filming for *The Outlaw Josey Wales* (the story is based on the Forrest Carter novel) was done in southern Utah at the beautiful Old Pariah location. The cinematography by Bruce Surtees is exceptional, but of course he had the striking southern Utah scenery to help him. The picture was directed by Eastwood. Anyone who has ever been the subject of a gross injustice (who hasn't?) will be able vicariously to avenge the wronged in watching this film.

THE KANAB AND ZION COUNTRY

During the 1930s, Kanab was often referred to as "Little Hollywood" for the many cowboy and feature films shot in the area. Today, about all that remains of this era is the "Frontier Movie Town" (297 West Center, Kanab), which features a movie set (period Western town), museum, and several partial sets from big-screen productions. Some of the first films in Utah, such as Tom Mix's 1924 *Deadwood Coach*, were filmed in the picturesque Kanab Canyon area northwest of town (4

miles north on U.S. 89, turn east and follow the access road into the Kanab Creek Canyon). A movie town was later built at the Kanab Canyon site, remnants of which can still be found several miles up the access road. Film companies also utilized the area now designated as the Coral Pink Sand Dunes State Park southwest of Kanab (drive north on U.S. 89 for 13 miles and then turn left or south on the dunes access road; follow this road south roughly 10 miles). Such films as *Arabian Nights* (1942, with Leif Erickson, Jon Hall, and Maria Montez) were filmed on the sand dunes. Another popular filming location around Kanab was the ghost town of Grafton (about 42 miles west of Kanab on State Route 9), which is set along the scenic Virgin River.

One of the better films to feature the landscape in the vicinity of Kanab during the "Golden Age of Film" was *Buffalo Bill* (1944), which starred Joel McCrea as Buffalo Bill, Maureen O'Hara as Louise Cody, and, if you look hard enough, future two-time Academy Award–winner Anthony Quinn (*Viva Zapata!*, 1952 and *Lust for Life*, 1956) as Yellow Hand. The river battle (the best scene in the film from a technical standpoint) was actually filmed on Kanab Creek (with a small dam to back the water up). Director William A. Wellman (a decorated veteran of World War I) had one year earlier directed the film version of *The Ox-Bow Incident* and would later direct *Track of the Cat* (1954).

With the advent of television, several weekly series were shot regularly in the Kanab Canyon area, including *Gunsmoke, Have Gun Will Travel,* and *Death Valley Days*. Still later came such films as *Sergeants Three* (1962), which starred the "Rat Pack" (first named by Humphrey Bogart)—Frank Sinatra, Sammy Davis, Jr., and Dean Martin—as three sergeants sent to a remote frontier outpost, where they have to employ a great deal of comic ingenuity to survive. Lifelong Kanab resident Jacquie Hamblin Rife, in an interview with the author, still recalled fondly how Sammy Davis, Jr., during the filming of *Sergeants Three,* traded her son dancing lessons for lessons with the lariat. After about

The Kanab Canyon area was used extensively by filmmakers during "The Golden Age of Film," but was also used for GUNSMOKE *(CBS, 1955–1975) and other television series. Courtesy John Murray.*

1960, as Westerns were replaced by other forms of action movies, shooting around Kanab subsided. There were still periods of excitement, though, as in the fall of 1968 when Director George Roy Hill brought his production of *Butch Cassidy and the Sundance Kid* to Grafton, just over the mountain from Kanab.

Butch Cassidy and the Sundance Kid

It's not often that a modern Western wins three Academy Awards, but *Butch Cassidy and the Sundance Kid* did just that: Best Script, Best Cinematography, and Best Song ("Raindrops Keep Fallin' on My Head"). The film was also nominated for two others (Best Director and Best Film). In addition to this *Butch Cassidy and the Sundance Kid* was one of the most successful movies of 1969 at the box office, grossing over $30 million—all in the same year that sixty-two-year-old John

OPPOSITE: *Clint Eastwood directs and plays the lead role of Josey Wales, a former Confederate soldier who is avenging the murder of his family, in* THE OUTLAW JOSEY WALES *(Warner Bros., 1976). Courtesy Photofest.*

Robert Redford

The name of Robert Redford will forever be associated with the deserts and mountains, rivers and canyons, mesas and buttes, arches and arroyos, slickrock and sagebrush of his adopted state, Utah. No other member of the motion picture community has ever been so committed to preserving the imperiled landscapes of the American West. When President Clinton stood on the South Rim of the Grand Canyon in September 1995 and signed the executive order creating the new 1.8 million acre Grand Staircase–Canyons of the Escalante National Monument, Redford was nearby, having played a quiet but active role in advancing the much needed proposal. Wherever there has been an environmental battle on the Colorado Plateau in need of a leader, Redford has been there, working hard to protect the unique scenery that is not only a vital part of American cinema, but also an essential component of American democracy.

Charles Robert Redford, Jr., was born on August 18, 1937, in Santa Monica, California. After a brief stint at the University of Colorado, Boulder, on a baseball scholarship Redford moved to Europe in 1957 to study painting (as did film director John Huston early in his life). A year later Redford returned to New York to further pursue both art and his newfound passion, acting. He made his stage debut in 1959 in a Broadway play, *Tall Story*. Four years later his lucky break came with a lead role in the Broadway comedy hit *Barefoot in the Park*. Soon Redford began appearing in popular television programs. Redford regularly played small parts on television and in film through the 1960s. He was abruptly catapulted to stardom following the success of *Butch Cassidy and the Sundance Kid* (1969). The film was shot on location in southeastern Utah (at Grafton, a ghost town in the vicinity of Zion National Park) and in southern Colorado (Animas Canyon near Durango). There followed such popular films as *Downhill Racer* (shot at Loveland Ski Basin in Colorado), *Jeremiah Johnson* (shot in Provo Canyon in Utah), and *The Electric Horseman* (also shot at the Grafton, Utah, site, as well as in Reno, Nevada). Surprisingly, Redford's Oscar came not for acting but for directing (*Ordinary People*, 1980). More recently, he has focused on films that are as much a revelation of wild nature as they are of human nature, including *A River Runs Through It* (1994) and *The Horse Whisperer* (1998). All of this is not bad for an accountant's son from southern California who could just as easily have followed in his father's professional footsteps. The fact that Redford chose what the poet Robert Frost called "The Road Not Taken" has forever changed the face of cinema, and the landscapes of the Southwest.

Robert Redford as the Sundance Kid in George Hill's BUTCH CASSIDY AND THE SUNDANCE KID *(20th-Fox, 1969). Courtesy Eddie Brandt's Saturday Matinee.*

Wayne won his first Oscar (for portraying federal marshal Rooster Cogburn in *True Grit*). Seen at the distance of several decades, the film seems particularly reflective of its turbulent time, as a pair of affable outlaws were cast as popular anti-heroes. The film came out during a year when anti-war dissidents were becoming cultural anti-heroes as they demonstrated against the Vietnam War. In this sense, the film, one of the first major anti-Westerns, became a subversive allegory used by its makers to protest, obliquely, government policy (with rail baron E. R. Harriman representing President Richard Nixon).

In a documentary entitled *The Making of Butch Cassidy and the Sundance Kid* director George Roy Hill recounts that the film took a difficult fifteen months to complete and that it was a continually developing project, involving considerable creative input from both Paul Newman (Butch Cassidy) and Robert Redford (the Sundance Kid). Early on a decision was made to humanize the two central characters as much as possible. Newman observed that he kept the character of Butch "very loose"—similar to the character of Cool Hand Luke, and the opposite of previous film characters he had played "tight" (such as Hud). He admitted to putting a "good deal of myself in the part." Sundance, on the other hand, was portrayed by Redford as "aloof, a loner." He was as quiet, brooding, and nervous as Newman's Butch Cassidy was outgoing, spontaneous, and fun-loving. Together the two formed a recognizable pair of friends, as opposites often unite to form that most basic human molecule.

Much of the early part of the film was shot on location in southwestern Utah at Grafton, a deserted Mormon community on the Virgin River near Zion National Park (6 miles west of Springdale on State Route 9). The surrounding scenery—much of it to the north actually in Zion National Park—provided a spectacular backdrop. An abandoned adobe church in the ghost town was converted into a schoolhouse, and one other structure was built, but the rest of the landscape remained unchanged. The film was shot at this location in October and November of 1968, and the autumn foliage along the Virgin River was at its lovely peak—yellow cottonwoods, orange alders, and russet-red scrub oak

Paul Newman as Butch Cassidy and Robert Redford as the Sundance Kid portray affable outlaws in George Hill's BUTCH CASSIDY AND THE SUNDANCE KID *(20th-Fox, 1969). Courtesy Photofest.*

(all against that chromium-blue Utah sky). It was at the Grafton site that one of the three musical sequences were shot, (Paul Newman playing on the bicycle with schoolteacher Edda Place (Katharine Ross) to Burt Bacharach's Oscar-winning lyric "Raindrops Keep Fallin' on My Head"). Director Hill opted for a more modern score in the film, as opposed to traditional period music, because he believed the characters were more contemporary in their carefree outlook and rebellious manner of living.

Viewers will note that the film has a washed-out, almost bleached quality—this results, according to the documentary, from the cinematographer (who would also win an Oscar) regularly shooting into sunny, backlit landscapes; intentionally overexposing the film two or three stops; and introducing a lot of dust and smoke into the scenes to create a slightly hazy effect. Also, many shots of the actors are through objects—such as foliage—which makes the audience actively search for the characters, and also pay closer attention to the action and especially to the dialogue. Parts of the film were also shot in the Animas Canyon north of Durango, Colorado (see Colorado chapter), and in the tropical highlands between Acapulco and Mexico City (the Bolivian sequence).

The last image in the film—during the climactic gunfight with the Bolivian Army—was, according to Director Hill, actually shot with an 8 x 10 large-format camera. The black-and-white image, slowly tinged with sepia as the shooting went on and on, quietly created an abstract, nostalgic closing for the film. Contrast this with the violent, up-close, slow motion deaths of Faye Dunaway and Warren Beatty in *Bonnie and Clyde* (1968). Like that other influential Western, *Stagecoach* (1939), *Butch Cassidy* has become a virtual anthology of innovative cinematic techniques that have since been widely emulated and imitated.

Recently the American Film Institute listed *Butch Cassidy and the Sundance Kid* as one of the one hundred most influential films of the twentieth century. In this respect, it was one of only a handful of other films with Southwestern settings—*Stagecoach* (1939), *The Grapes of Wrath* (1940), *The Treasure of the Sierra Madre* (shot in Mexico, 1948), *High Noon* (1952), *Giant* (1956), *The Searchers* (1956), *Bonnie and Clyde* (1967), and *Easy Rider* (1969)—so honored. It seems certain that *Butch Cassidy and the Sundance Kid* will endure, both because it is so representative of an axial moment in American history, and because it tells a good story with strong characters so well (more easily said than done).

Other Locations in Utah

Butch Cassidy Home (5 miles south of Circleville on U.S. 89)— Butch Cassidy (whose real name was Robert Leroy Parker) was a real-life historical character. His home can still be seen in the midst of the beautiful southern Utah landscape where he made the legend that was later immortalized in the 1969 film *Butch Cassidy and the Sundance Kid*. Butch Cassidy's sister publicly stated in her later years that he had not been killed in Bolivia, but had actually returned to the United States and lived under an assumed identity.

Sundance Film Institute (P.O Box 16450, Salt Lake City, 84116)—Every year Robert Redford's Sundance Film Institute previews the work of independent filmmakers at the Sundance Festival in Park City in mid-January. The respected festival attracts major actors, directors, producers, and critics.

Goblin Valley State Park (located about 40 miles south of Interstate 70, exit 147, via State Route 24)—Goblin Valley State Park has redrock formations every bit as striking as those found in Arches National Park and Canyonlands National Park, with one advantage—it is a remote and little-visited state park (meaning that film permits are easier to obtain). The park has been featured in films such as *City Slickers* (1991).

Moab to Monument Valley Film Museum (Moab)— Located in downtown Moab (50 East Center, #1), and always attended by the affable Kari Murphy, the museum is a great place to learn more about the rich film history of the area. The museum includes movie posters, stills, and props.

Provo (located about 40 miles south of the state capitol of Salt Lake City, via Interstate 15)—The film *Footloose* (with Christopher Penn, Sarah Jessica Parker, and John Lithgow, 1984), which featured Kevin Bacon in the early stages of his career, was partly filmed in Provo, including the flour mill which can be seen from the Lehi exit of Interstate 15. Robert Redford's popular ski resort Sundance (located east of Provo via U.S. 189 and State Route 92) served as one of the locations for his 1972 film *Jeremiah Johnson*, based on Vardis Fisher's novel *Mountain Man*. Parts of the film were also shot in the nearby Uinta National Forest.

Robert Redford as Jeremiah Johnson is a man who becomes disenchanted with civilization and moves to the wilderness in Sydney Pollack's JEREMIAH JOHNSON *(Warner Bros., 1972). Courtesy Eddie Brandt's Saturday Matinee.*

COLORADO

any people who have traveled the length and breadth of the Rocky Mountains believe that the most impressive section of the great cordillera (which begins in the Yukon and ends south of Santa Fe) is in Colorado. No other state has as much high country. More than 70 percent of the nation's land above 10,000 feet is found within the state, which has an average altitude of nearly 7,000 feet. Fifty-three peaks in the state have summits greater than 14,000 feet, and over two hundred are higher than 13,000 feet. In their power and grace, the peaks of Colorado have often been compared to those of the Alps. In fact, the southern mountains of the state around Ouray and Silverton—the heart of the San Juan Range—is often referred to as "Little Switzerland." There are peaks in Colorado that are as striking as Mount Fuji (the Spanish Peaks near Walsenburg), and others, like the Maroon Bells near Aspen, that match anything in the national parks of Alberta. With twelve national forests and twenty-two million acres of forested land, fifty thousand square miles of antelope prairie and redrock country as lovely as anything in Arizona, Colorado offers filmmakers an incredibly rich array of natural landscapes.

When the legendary Tom Mix launched his filmmaking career in 1910, it was in the rugged canyon country near Canon City, Colorado. Between 1910 and 1917 he appeared in over one hundred one- and two-

Tom Mix as Tom Gordon works undercover as a highwayman to stop a string of train robberies in Lewis Seiler's THE GREAT K & A TRAIN ROBBERY *(Fox, 1926). Courtesy Photofest.*

reelers, and many of them were shot in this classic western landscape along the Arkansas River. Part of the reason for shooting in Colorado was that the motion picture films of the time required quite a bit of natural light, and intense sunlight is a commodity found in abundance at high altitude. One of Mix's best films—*The Great K & A Train Robbery* (1926)— was filmed at Royal Gorge and at Glenwood Canyon. (In the guise of a bandit, Tom Mix discovers that the robberies are an inside job and also manages to fall in love with the daughter of the train owner.)

By the late 1920s the film industry had consolidated itself in Hollywood, but Colorado still was was still used regularly as a field location. This was increasingly the case after World War II, when such films as *Across the Wide Missouri* (with Clark Gable and Ricardo Montalban, 1951), *Lone Star* (with Clark Gable, Ava Gardner, and

OPPOSITE: *The Wilson Peaks area served as a geographic and aesthetic anchor for* TRUE GRIT *(Paramount, 1969). Courtesy John Murray.*

Bruce Willis as Detective John McClane is in a race against time while trying to stop terrorists who are killing airline passengers in Renny Harlin's DIE HARD 2 *(20th-Fox, 1990). Courtesy Eddie Brandt's Saturday Matinee.*

Kid. The country through which they pass is renowned for its grandeur. The San Juan Mountains continue to be a favorite filming area, and have appeared in such classics as *How the West Was Won* (1962), *True Grit* (see below), *The Cowboys* (1972), and *City Slickers* (1990). Many films have also utilized the mountains and ski resorts around Denver, most notably Robert Redford's film *Downhill Racer* (1970) and *National Lampoon's Vacation* (1982). More recently, filmmakers have been utilizing the extensive indoor studios that were built at the site of the old Denver Stapleton airport (also the former site of Bruce Willis' 1990 blockbuster *Die Hard 2*).

Colorado offers filmmakers scenery that can be found nowhere else in the Southwest. It is a country that takes one's breath away, both figuratively and literally. There is no wilder country south of the Canadian border (a grizzly bear nearly killed a man in the San Juan mountains in 1979), and there are landscapes the likes of which can not be surpassed anywhere in the world. A century of filmmaking has created a body of work that pays quiet tribute to the timeless beauty that is Colorado.

Lionel Barrymore), *Denver and Rio Grande* (with Sterling Hayden, 1952), *Naked Spur* (with Jimmy Stewart, 1953), and *The Siege at Red River* (with Van Johnson and Richard Boone, 1954) were shot in the state. Almost all of these films were shot around Durango, in La Plata County, and in Ouray County just to the north—among the most picturesque mountains in the state.

As the years have passed, Colorado has proven itself one of the most popular filming locations in the Southwest. The Cumbres & Toltec Railroad (which runs from Antonito, Colorado, to Chama, New Mexico) and the Durango-Silverton Narrow Gauge (which runs from Durango to Silverton) have appeared in several major films, including *Indiana Jones and the Last Crusade* and *Butch Cassidy and the Sundance*

Cat Ballou

In many ways, *Cat Ballou* (1965), with its satiric and good-natured spoofing of the Western genre, prepared the way for *Butch Cassidy and the Sundance Kid* four years later (as well as, in 1974, for *Blazing Saddles*). Both *Cat Ballou* and *Butch Cassidy* involved lovable outlaws during the twilight years of the frontier who blunder through a series of picaresque episodes including train holdups, horse chases, dusty trails, bordellos, thwarted love, and a "Hole in the Wall" hideout (although *Cat Ballou* has a brighter ending). From the first lines of dialogue in *Cat Ballou*—Jane Fonda (as Cat Ballou): "Hello, I'm Katherine Ballou." / Dwayne Hickman (as Jed): "I'm drunk as a skunk."—the audience understands this will not be a serious western, a la *Fort*

OPPOSITE: *Jane Fonda as Cat Ballou is saddled up with Michael Callan as Clay Boone in Elliot Silverstein's western spoof* CAT BALLOU *(Columbia, 1965). Courtesy Eddie Brandt's Saturday Matinee.*

Lee Marvin

Throughout the 1950s and 1960s, whenever Hollywood needed a "heavy" in a major picture, they called on Lee Marvin. The tall, lean, ruggedly handsome ex-Marine could always be counted on to carry the role. In picture after picture, Marvin established a classic ambiance simply by walking through the barroom doors or riding a horse into town. He was Hector David in *Bad Day at Black Rock*, with a cast that included Spencer Tracy and Walter Brennan; Crow in *The Comancheros*, with a cast that included John Wayne and Stuart Whitman; and Ben Rumson in *Paint Your Wagon*, with a cast that included Clint Eastwood and Jean Sebert. Marvin was the quintessential working actor of the era, and not only in Westerns—he also appeared regularly in serious dramas *(Ship of Fools)*, crime melodramas *(The Killers)*, and war films *(The Dirty Dozen, The Big Red One)*.

Born in 1924 in New York City, the son of an advertising executive and a fashion writer, Marvin began acting after returning from military service, first on the Broadway stage (he appeared in the 1951 production of *Billy Bud*) and later in films *(You're in the Navy Now)*. Over the next decade his career grew slowly but steadily. His crowning achievement occurred in 1965 with an Oscar for his dual-role performance (Kid Shellen/Tim Strawn) in *Cat Ballou*. The film was shot in the mountains near Canon City, Colorado. Lee Marvin, who loved the Southwest landscapes, actually lived there—he designed and built a home in the desert outside Tucson, Arizona, where he lived until his death.

Unlike many Hollywood actors who have played heroes, Lee Marvin actually was one. Wounded as an infantry rifleman during a battle on Guadalcanal, Marvin is today buried in Arlington National Cemetary in Washington, D.C. On the gravestone is a simple inscription: "Lee Marvin 1924–1987, Private, United States Marine Corps, World War II, Pacific Theater, Purple Heart."

Lee Marvin earned an Academy Award for his dual, comedic performances as the drunken Tim Strawn and noted gunfighter, Kid Shelleen in Elliot Silverstein's CAT BALLOU *(Columbia, 1965). Courtesy Eddie Brandt's Saturday Matinee.*

Apache (1948) or *Shane* (1953). The presence of Nat King Cole (in his final screen appearance), playing a banjo and singing folk ballads, also assured an informal ambiance.

The plot is one of the oldest and most successful in the Western—a young female schoolteacher arrives back at her father's cattle ranch to discover the bad guys have taken over the valley. She hires a gunfighter—as in Akira Kurosawa's *The Seven Samurai* (1954) and later in John Sturges' *The Magnificent Seven* (1960)—and proceeds to do battle. What makes this film unique is its radical recasting of the hero (the gunfighter). Instead of A. B. Guthrie's cool-headed, virtuous gunfighter Shane, played by Allan Ladd in that influential film, we have a chronically drunk, manically unstable, Falstaffian figure in the form of Lee Marvin (the original Western anti-hero). The screen lines that Marvin was given in this film are superb, and helped him to build the role into the Oscar-winner that it was. His acting throughout—both the rendering of the script and the physical comedy—is entirely worthy of the honor it received (which is not always the case). This is one of the few films made in the sixties—one thinks also of Stanley Kubrick's *Dr. Strangelove* (1964)—that can still make a viewer laugh out loud in the twenty-first century. The film also featured an underrated performance by twenty-eight-year-old Jane Fonda, who, together with Lee Marvin, literally held the film together with powerful, inspired acting and helped propel it into significance. She would later win Oscars for both *Julia* (1977) and *Coming Home* (1978).

Cat Ballou was shot in Fremont and Custer counties in southcentral Colorado. The filming took place in October 1964 at two locations: the Buckskin Film Set near Canon City and the upper Wet Mountain Valley near Westcliffe. All of the sequences in "Wolf City, Wyoming" were filmed at the Buckskin Film Set (drive 8 miles west of Canon City on U.S. 50, then, following the signs, turn left on County Road 3A and follow for 1 mile). The Buckskin site, though private, is open to the public as a historical filming site from Memorial Day through Labor Day. Situated on about a quarter-section of land near the Royal Gorge of the Arkansas River, Buckskin consists of reconstructed mining-era log buildings that approximate a frontier town of the late nineteenth century. It has been used regularly for films and for television over the years. It has more of a rustic ambiance than the film set at Paramount Ranch in the Santa Monica National Recreation Area (see California chapter) or the film set at Old Tucson (see Arizona chapter). The Wet Mountain Valley, where the ranching sequences were shot, can be reached by driving about 15 miles west of Canon City on U.S. 50 to the junction with State Route 69. Turn left, or south, on State Route 69 and drive about 20 miles to Westcliffe. This is one of the loveliest mountain valleys in Colorado, with the Sangre de Cristo Range toward the west and the Wet Mountains to the east.

One of the axioms of psychology is that large social groups, including countries, behave much as individuals do. Fear, guilt, anger, hope, happiness, pride—all are as common to nations as to people. Seen from the perspective of many decades, it is clear that the cluster of successful comedic films like Cat Ballou in the mid-sixties—one thinks as well of *A Hard Day's Night* (1964), *Help!* (1965), *What's New, Pussycat?* (1965), *The Pink Panther* (1964) and, again, of *Dr. Strangelove*—helped the grieving nation cheer itself up after the assassination of President Kennedy in 1963. These comedic films were, in a way, its best medicine.

True Grit

When Mattie Ross (played by Kim Darby) first meets Rooster Cogburn (John Wayne), she asks, "Mr. Cogburn, can I talk with you for a minute? They tell me you're a man with true grit." Rooster pauses in the courthouse stairway, looks skeptically up at her through his one good eye (the other covered by a black eye patch), and so this colorful, moving, Oscar-winning story of two real characters in the Old West begins. Darby is the only child of a prominent cattle rancher who has been gunned down by an outlaw. She is determined to see the perpetrator hanged. Cogburn is the notorious federal marshal who has killed twenty-three fugitives in four years (for which he has just been reprimanded by a liberal judge concerned about the constitutional rights of criminals). An eccentric curmudgeon, Rooster lives in the back of

Glen Campbell (La Bouef), John Wayne (Rooster Cogburn), and Kim Darby (Mattie Ross) become an unlikely trio in search of revenge in Henry Hathaway's TRUE GRIT *(Paramount, 1969). Courtesy Eddie Brandt's Saturday Matinee.*

Chuen-sen's grocery store with his house cat, General Sterling Pride. He is always looking for easy money and has found no better way to obtain it than hunting down worthless outlaws and collecting the bounties. Soon a Texas Ranger, played by Glen Campbell (a popular singer of the 1960s), wanders into the story. Campbell is hoping to collect the Texas reward on the same outlaw, who has previously killed a popular U.S. Senator in Texas (Campbell then plans to marry the daughter of the Senator). Within a day, the three light out for the territories.

What follows is one of the most memorable tales in the history of Southwestern film. Alternately serious and comic, irreverent and respectful of the genre, *True Grit* succeeds primarily because it is built so carefully on the three fundamentals of Southwestern film: brilliant characters, a strong story line, and magnificent scenery. Along the way, as in all good dramas, each central character undergoes significant changes. Wayne discovers his tender human side as he takes on Kim Darby as a kind of surrogate daughter, and Kim Darby finds an inner toughness as she sticks close to her newly adopted father, and learns a lot about the world from him. Texas Ranger Glen Campbell, the least savvy and weakest member of the triangle, is gunned down and dies in the final shoot-out. The film includes the only performance of John Wayne ever to win an Oscar. At this stage of his career—with over one hundred films to his credit—Wayne had the weathered, character-filled face of a range bull. Having established himself as the premier Western actor of the century, he was not afraid to make fun of himself or the genre along the way. His last line in the film, before he gallops off to new adventures, is hilarious: "Well, come see a fat old man sometime!"

True Grit also includes fine secondary performances by future Oscar-winner Robert Duvall (Tender Mercies, 1983) and by the versatile Dennis Hopper, who by this time in his career had appeared in such films as *Rebel Without a Cause* (1955), *Giant* (1956), *Gunfight at the O.K. Corral* (1957), *Hang 'Em High* (1968) and *Easy Rider* (1969, which he also directed). The film was directed by Henry Hathaway, whose credits then included *The Lives of a Bengal Lancer* (1935), *Sundown*

(1941), *How the West Was Won* (three episodes, 1962), *The Sons of Katie Elder* (1965), and *Nevada Smith* (1966).

True Grit was shot in October1968 in Southwestern Colorado (San Miguel and Ouray Counties). Coincidentally, this was the same month and year that director George Roy Hill was filming another Oscar-winning western, *Butch Cassidy and the Sundance Kid*, not far away, at Grafton in southwestern Utah (see Utah chapter). The area in which *True Grit* was filmed includes some of the highest country in Colorado (near the ski resort of Telluride). Wayne, who only had one lung, can be seen struggling to catch his breath in some of the scenes, particularly in those scenes requiring physical action without a stunt double or with any extended dialogue (portable oxygen tanks were on the set at all times).

The first image in the film is of the Wilson Peaks, which are three closely related 14,000-foot mountains (Mount Wilson, El Diente, and Wilson Peak) in the San Miguel Range. These three towering peaks—Colorado's version of the Grand Tetons—serve as a geographic and aesthetic anchor for *True Grit*. They appear in more outdoor scenes than any other landscape feature, and their presence is almost that of an unspoken character in the film. Most of the shots of the Wilson Peaks in the film were taken from Wilson Mesa, which is about 6 miles due north of the Wilson Peaks Massif (drive west on State Route 145 from Telluride about 10 miles and then turn left, or south, on 60 Mile Road at Vanadium). Some of the later scenes were shot at The Meadows, which are located on the south side of the range (drive south from Telluride over Lizard Head Pass on State Route 145 for about 20 miles and then turn right or west on Forest Service Road 535; follow about 4 miles).

After Darby leaves her family ranch (the footage of which was shot at an old homestead along Big Bear Creek on Wilson Mesa) the action shifts to a small frontier town where her father's murder took place. This entire sequence was shot in and around the town square of Ridgeway, Colorado (11 miles north of Ouray on U.S. 550). Most notable is the old courthouse building, where Kim Darby and John

Wayne first have a conversation. Many identifiable buildings can be seen in the film, although some temporary sets were built (such as the corral where Kim Darby bargains with the horse trader) and then removed after shooting. Subsequently, the ferry sequence was shot at Blue Mesa Resevoir (38 miles east of Montrose on U.S. 50). Considerable action, in the early pursuit phase, then takes place in the vicinity of Owl Creek Pass (drive north of Ridgeway 6 miles on U.S. 550 and then turn right on Forest Service Road 8 to Owl Creek Pass). Most of the final action occurs back on Wilson Mesa.

    True Grit is, simply put, one of the most enjoyable films ever made. A fatherless young woman finds a new dad and a cantankerous old bachelor finds the daughter he never had. Everything that John Wayne had learned over the previous half century went into his acting in this film, and the result was an immortal creation: Rooster Cogburn. Five years later Wayne resurrected the role in *Rooster Cogburn* (1974), a film shot in Oregon with Katherine Hepburn as the incorrigible spinster Eula Goodnight. No film has better featured the magnificent landscapes of the Colorado high country. As can be seen in this picture, the high country of the southern Rockies is most beautiful in the fall, with the quaking aspen turning bright yellow, the scrub oak a warm rust-red, and over it all a high altitude sky so deep blue as to be almost purple.

Other Locations in Colorado

Boulder (Boulder is located about 20 miles northwest of Denver, via U.S. 36)—The home at 1619 Pine Street was the house in which Robin Williams and Pam Dawber lived in the ABC sitcom *Mork and Mindy* (a popular program in the late seventies). A frequently used location in the show was the New York Deli (on the Boulder Mall, at 1117 Pearl Street). Additionally, some scenes for Woody Allen's film *Sleeper* (1974) were filmed at the futuristic-looking National Center for Atmospheric Research (designed by famed architect I. M. Pei) in south Boulder (follow Table Mesa Drive west as far as you can—the large mountain park area with the lovely red-bricked buildings integrated

Colorado's jagged peaks were used as a backdrop for DOWNHILL RACER *(Wildwood, 1969). Courtesy John Murray.*

into the landscape is N.C.A.R.). Another site in the foothills area that was used for *Sleeper* was the striking "bubble-home" (made of polyurethane foam sprayed over metal forms) on Genessee Mountain west of Denver (follow I-70 west of the Morrison exit about 8 miles—the distinctive white egg-shaped home is located about a half mile south of the interstate on an exposed point).

RED ROCKS COUNTY PARK (1 mile north of Morrison along State Route 2 in Jefferson County just west of Denver)—Parts of *Ford Fairlane* (1989), with Andrew Dice Clay, were shot in Red Rocks. This park includes the world-renowned Red Rocks outdoor musical amphitheater, in which such great musical acts as The Beatles, Bruce Springsteen and the "E" Street Band, The Clash, and U2 have played. If you watch VH-1 or MTV long enough, you will see a tape of the famous performance that U2 gave early in their career at Red Rocks during a soaking rain storm. Some think, the author included, that this was the finest performance the band ever gave. The award for best performance *ever* at Red Rocks, though, goes, naturally, to the Boss, Bruce Springsteen (1980).

SID KING'S BURLESQUE HOUSE (northwest corner of Ogden and Colfax in Denver)—Sid King's burlesque house (still the same sort of business but under new management) appeared in Clint Eastwood's 1978 comedy film *Every Which Way But Loose*.

ESTES PARK (about 30 miles northwest of Boulder, via U.S. 36)—Stephen King, the Edgar Allen Poe of our time, worked as a maintenance man at the Stanley Hotel—the sprawling white Victorian-era resort on the north side of town—during his down-and-out years. He mined this experience, and location, for background material while writing his novel *The Shining* (with Jack Nicholson, 1980), a film that built on the previous success of *Carrie* (1976).

LOVELAND SKI RESORT (about 50 miles west of Denver on I-70)—Robert Redford filmed much of his skiing picture *Downhill Racer* at Loveland (one of the friendliest ski resorts in Colorado, and with some of the nicest intermediate terrain).

BRECKENRIDGE (about 70 miles west of Denver via I-70 and then State Route 9)—*National Lampoon's Christmas Vacation* (1980) was shot partly in the ski resort town of Breckenridge.

Clint Eastwood as Philo Beddoe is a brawling, truck driver who fights his way out of countless situations with a whole cast of bad guys in James Fargo's comedy EVERY WHICH WAY BUT LOOSE *(Warner Bros., 1978). Courtesy Photofest.*

GUNNISON (about 60 miles east of Monroe on U.S. 50)—The sequence in *The Searchers* (1956) in which John Wayne massacres the buffalo was shot on a private ranch (exact location unknown) in the upper Gunnison Valley.

GRAND JUNCTION (about 240 miles west of Denver on I-70)—Some of the early scenes of *Thelma and Louise* (see Utah chapter) were shot on highways and backroads in the Grand Junction area, including U.S. 50, State Route 139, and State Route 141 (including the small town of Bedrock in Paradox Valley).

PAGOSA SPRINGS (62 miles east of Durango on U.S. 160)—John Wayne's classic 1972 film *The Cowboys* (one of the few films in which his character dies), was filmed on private ranches in the San Juan Valley of Archuleta County.

WOLF CREEK PASS (30 miles southwest of South Fork on U.S. 160)—In *National Lampoon's Vacation* (1983), the Clarke Griswold family spends the night at the last major RV-cabin-camping-fishing-pond resort on the eastern approach to the pass (located on the south side of the road, the resort changes names frequently).

CUMBRES & TOLTEC NARROW GAUGE RAIL LINE (runs between Antonito, Colorado, and Chama, New Mexico)—The initial rail sequences in *Indiana Jones and the Last Crusade* (1989) were shot on this popular rail line which runs through the southern San Juan Mountains.

DURANGO-SILVERTON NARROW GAUGE RAIL LINE (connects the old-time mining village of Silverton—made famous in the art world by an Ansel Adams print—with the modern boomtown of Durango)—This historic rail line made its best-known appearance in *Butch Cassidy and the Sundance Kid* (1969, see below). Other major films include *Ticket to Tomahawk* (with Marilyn Monroe and Walter Brennan, 1950), *Denver and Rio Grande* (with Sterling Hayden and Dean Jagger, 1952), *Viva Zapata* (with Marlon Brando and Anthony Quinn, who won a best-acting Oscar for the film, 1952), *Run for Cover* (with James Cagney, Ernest Borgnine, and John Derek, 1955), and *How the West Was Won* (with Debbie Reynolds, Gregory Peck, and many other luminaries, 1962) and *Bite the Bullet* (with Oscar-winners Gene Hackman and Ben

Johnson, as well as James Coburn, who would finally, after sixty films, win his Oscar for *Affliction* in 1999, 1975).

DURANGO (45 miles east of Cortez on U.S. 160)—Some key scenes in Billy Crystal's surprisingly successful Western *City Slickers* (1990) were shot on private ranches northwest of town (Lightner Creek, 5 miles west of Durango on U.S. 160, accessed by County Road 207). Durango has been used regularly for filming since the silent era (such now-forgotten Westerns as the 1919 film *Mesa Verde*).

LOWER ANIMAS CANYON (located about 10 miles north of Durango on U.S. 550 via County Road 250)—Two key sequences in *Butch Cassidy and the Sundance Kid* (1969) were shot in the Lower Animas Canyon north of Durango: the first scene in the film (the train robbery) and the later scene in which Redford and Newman jump from a cliff into a river. Although the first part of the cliff-jump scene (the beginning of the jump with the real actors) was shot on the west side of the Lower Animas Canyon, the latter part of it (the completion of the jump) was shot with stunt doubles on a movie ranch in the Santa Monica Mountains near Hollywood. The two shots were then edited together to produce the smooth action now seen in the film (all this according to director George Roy Hill in Robert L. Crawford's documentary *The Making of Butch Cassidy and the Sundance Kid*).

OPPOSITE: *Daniel Stern (Phil Berquist), Billy Crystal (Mitch Robbins), and Bruno Kirby (Ed Furillo) are three close city friends on a roundup in Ron Underwood's* CITY SLICKERS *(Columbia, 1991). Courtesy Eddie Brandt's Saturday Matinee.*

NEW MEXICO

New Mexico is the state that perhaps best embodies the diverse landscapes and images, legends and myths, histories and mysteries, tragedies and triumphs, parables and paradoxes of the American West. Here are the striking mountain scenes that so inspired the Taos Seven artists, the Rio Grande and Pecos river valleys with their prosperous ranching communities, and the hot, dry border country with Mexico. Across it all—canyons and rivers, deserts and mountains, forests and prairies almost without end—flows that famous wash of high-altitude New Mexico light. This is the same light that so dazzled D. H. Lawrence and Willa Cather, Eliot Porter and Ansel Adams, Ernest Blumenschein and T. C. Cannon. Although hard and metallic at high noon, the upland light grows otherwordly at dawn and dusk. Blue shadows arise and complex shapes become clearly defined. Clouds reveal their immaculate depths and heights. Earth tones warm and the land truly awakens from its slumber. It is the magical time of day, and the extraordinary sort of place, that artists and photographers, poets and philosophers, actors and filmmakers live for.

From the beginning of filmmaking, the intense natural light and enchanting natural scenes of New Mexico have attracted filmmakers. And it is a surprisingly old history—more than a century at this writing. In fact, one of the first experimental films ever made—Thomas Edison's 1898 *Indian Day School*—was shot on location at Isleta Pueblo near Albuquerque. To put that date into historical perspective, future film director John Ford was still a little boy listening to picaresque stories in his father's saloon back on the East Coast, one-day Oscar winner John Wayne was just a twinkle in his father's eye, and New Mexico would not become a state for more than a decade.

What has followed that first experimental picture is the stuff of Academy Awards and Golden Globe Awards, countless Saturday matinees and drive-in theater shows. For the last one hundred years New Mexico has provided the setting for every genre known to American film, and virtually every actor of note—from Katharine Hepburn to Jodie Foster, Henry Fonda to Clint Eastwood, Spencer Tracy to Jack Nicholson—has performed his or her craft in New Mexico at some point in their career. A partial list of successful films based wholly or significantly in New Mexico reads like a history of film itself, from the original *Billy the Kid* to *Oklahoma!* to *Contact*. In New Mexico filmmakers have consistently found a series of landscapes that can provide the stage for virtually any story the human imagination can conceive.

OPPOSITE: *The White Sands National Monument and surrounding area was used as a backdrop for* KING SOLOMON'S MINES *(MGM, 1950),* BITE THE BULLET *(Columbia, 1975), and* YOUNG GUNS II *(20th-Fox, 1990). Courtesy John Murray.*

Northern New Mexico

Northern New Mexico offers some of the most striking landscapes in the state—the southern terminus of the Rocky Mountains near Taos, the historic Pueblo communities, the highlands surrounding Los Alamos, the Rio Grande Gorge, the Rio Chama country, Shiprock and the Navajo Reservation, Las Vegas and the old Comanche grasslands to the east, and the open range landscapes south of Santa Fe. While there are abundant public resources for filmmaking—National Forests (Carson, Santa Fe, Cibola) and Bureau of Land Management land—there are also several private locations in the region designed specifically for that purpose. These include the Bonanza Creek Ranch, which was featured in such films as *The Man from Laramie* (1955, with Jimmy Stewart), *Cowboy* (1958, with Glenn Ford and Jack Lemmon), and *The Legend of the Lone Ranger* (1980, with Jason Robards); the Ghost Ranch near Abiquiu, which formed one of the many backdrops for *City Slickers* (1991, with Billy Crystal); the Cook Ranch (also known as the Silverado Set) south of Santa Fe, which was used for *Silverado* (1985, with Kevin Costner and Danny Glover) and *Lonesome Dove* (1989, with Robert Duvall and Tommy Lee Jones); and the Eaves Movie Ranch, also near Santa Fe, which can be seen in such films as *Chisum* (1970, with John Wayne) and *Wyatt Earp* (1994, with Kevin Costner and Gene Hackman). All but the Eaves Movie Ranch are closed to the public.

Other popular filming sites include the Cumbres & Toltec Scenic Railroad, an historic narrow-gauge rail line that runs forty miles from Chama, New Mexico, to Antonito, Colorado, as well as several of the Indian Pueblos (such as Zia pueblo near Albuquerque). Some of the best public places in the region to view film locations are the Santa Fe plaza *(Twins)*, Taos *(Easy Rider; Butch Cassidy and the Sundance Kid)*, Truchas *(The Milagro Beanfield War)*, the Cumbres & Toltec Scenic Railroad *(Indiana Jones and the Last Crusade)*, and the Rio Grande Gorge *(Natural Born Killers)*. Anyone touring this area should spend some time at the Indian pueblos, especially Taos Pueblo; Acoma, or the Sky City, west of Albuquerque (featured in *Sundown*); San Ildefonso Pueblo near Los Alamos (featured in *Lonesome Dove*); and Santo Domingo Pueblo near Bernalillo (featured in *Lonesome Dove*).

Northern New Mexico offers some of the finest filming country in the American Southwest. Even as this book went to press, preparations were being made to film another major motion picture, *All the Pretty Horses* (based on the Cormac McCarthy novel and directed by Oscar-winner Billy Bob Thornton) in the area. Another movie made in northern New Mexico, *Wild Wild West,* with Will Smith, was released. Since the silent-era days of Tom Mix, this beautiful region of the Southwest has served as a major filming location for the industry. Given its long and distinguished past, and the many unique resources that remain available, its future in this respect is secure.

Easy Rider

Easy Rider is one of the most controversial films ever made in the Southwest. It is also among the finest films ever to come from the region, as evidenced by its recent inclusion in the American Film Institute's compilation of the *One Hundred Best Films of the Twentieth Century.* In this unusual movie co-writers Dennis Hopper and Terry Southern (who also wrote the screenplays for such classic 1960 films as Stanley Kubrick's *Dr. Strangelove*) present an unflinching look at the alienated counterculture of the 1960s. The film follows two main characters—Billy (Dennis Hopper) and Captain America (Peter Fonda)—as they travel by Harley-Davidson motorcycle from Los Angeles across the Southwest to the Mardi Gras in New Orleans, Louisiana. This is not the simple and straightforward Old Southwest of Tom Mix and Gene Autry, John Ford and John Wayne. There are no comfortable myths or familiar illusions. The heroes ride motorcycles instead of horses. The American flag is not waving from a cavalry guidon but is stitched on the back of a leather jacket. The Indians are the "good guys" and the "bad guys" are the police. The desert is a place not of pitched battles but of quiet revelation. The world of *Easy Rider* is, from beginning to end, a world of anti-narrative and anti-hero, subculture and psychedelia, subtle metaphor and harsh satire.

Peter Fonda as Captain America is a long-haired LA biker in search of "the real America" on the road to New Orleans in Dennis Hopper's EASY RIDER *(Columbia, 1969). Courtesy Photofest.*

The film mocks, in artful ways, the traditions of filmmaking in the Southwest, as in the key transitional moment in which Billy (Dennis Hopper) and Captain America (Peter Fonda) ride their motorcycles over the Colorado River Bridge at Needles, California. The wide angle camera lens pans over the same stark desert mountains (the Chemehuevi Mountains) that appeared in a similarly pivotal scene thirty-eight years earlier in *The Grapes of Wrath*, a film that featured the Oscar-winning performance of Henry Fonda (Peter Fonda's father). In the earlier film, the main characters (the displaced Joads) were traveling west on Route 66 from the wasteland of the east to the hope-filled arcadia of southern California. In *Easy Rider,* the journey is reversed, with the characters traveling east down the same lonely highway from the bright Pacific coast back into the dark heart of America. Both films are successful pieces of social criticism, but the aesthetic approaches could not be more different.

Easy Rider may be a serious film, the story of a modern-day vision quest by a pair (later a trio) of errant mutant-knights in search of an idea (freedom), but it is also—and this partly explains why the film has endured as a work of art—an often comical story that never takes itself too seriously. One thinks especially, in this regard, of the hilarious campfire scene in which lawyer George Hanson (Jack Nicholson) sober-ly informs a gullible Billy (Dennis Hopper) that space aliens (he calls them Venusians) have infiltrated American society and are "living and breeding among us." Another joy is the sound track, with classic sixties songs by Bob Dylan ("It's Allright, Ma (I'm Only Bleeding)), Jimi Hendrix ("If Six Was Nine"), Steppenwolf ("The Pusher"), and Roger McGuinn and the Byrds ("Ballad of Easy Rider").

Throughout the film, the familiar landscapes of the American West are prominently featured, including Death Valley and the Mojave Desert along California state route 190 (where the dynamic duo camp the first night); the San Francisco Peaks north of Flagstaff, Arizona (where they take on the hitchhiker along U.S. 89 who leads them to Taos; they also stop at the Sacred Mountain gas station about 20 miles north of Flagstaff on U.S. 89); the monoliths of Monument Valley (where they camp in the Anasazi ruins for the night); and the Taos Pueblo and its environs (where they spend time on a commune with Karen Black and company). So enamored was Dennis Hopper with the scenery of northern New Mexico during the filming of *Easy Rider* that he actually purchased the D. H. Lawrence home north of Taos and lived in it for a time (the home is now owned and operated as a museum by the University of New Mexico).

The Taos Pueblo is the Southwest's tallest pueblo and was used in EASY RIDER *(Columbia, 1969) and other films. Courtesy John Murray.*

The Milagro Beanfield War

The Milagro Beanfield War (1988) is based on the popular novel by Taos writer John Nichols [the other two books in the trilogy are *The Nirvana Blues* (1978) and *The Magic Journey* (1981)]. The film was directed by Robert Redford, who had previously received an Oscar for directing *Ordinary People* (with Timothy Hutton, Mary Tyler Moore, and Donald Sutherland, 1980). Redford assembled a unique ensemble of novice, journeyman, and master actors to tell this rich and complex story of northern New Mexico, including Rubén Blades, Richard Bradford, Sonia Braga, John Heard, Julie Carmen, James Gammon, Daniel Stern, Chick Vennera, Christopher Walken, Freddy Fender (the country-western singer), Melanie Griffith, and Daniel Stern. The two primary characters in this sprawling cast are Chick Vennera, who portrays a

Carlos Riquelme as the indestructable Amarante Cordova walks with his pig, Lupita, in Robert Redford's THE MILAGRO BEANFIELD WAR *(Universal, 1987). Courtesy Photofest.*

The conflict centers on Chick Vennera's decision to water his family's historic beanfield, a piece of property which is now controlled by Ladd Devine. The beanfield occupies the middle of what will soon become the thirteenth fairway of the planned resort development. Nichols, and Redford, frame the story in classic dialectic terms—tradition versus progress, working-class values versus aristocratic values, the country versus the city, the family man versus the man with no family, the individual versus society. Along the way, Christopher Walken is brilliantly cast as the state police officer put in charge of neutralizing Chick Vennera. John Heard puts in a fine performance as the former ACLU lawyer who now edits the local paper, *La Voz del Norte*. The film takes good-natured shots at everyone—the self-serious forest service officials, the bumbling sheriff, the excitable townspeople, the incompetent governor, Ladd Devine's witless companion (Melanie Griffith), even Joe Mondragon (the impulsive anti-hero). In the end, *The Milagro Beanfield War* is a marvelous piece of magic realism (Nichols has been influenced by the Latin American master, Gabriel García Márquez). Like all good satires, it makes a serious point about the human condition in a gentle way.

One of the things that makes this film a delight to view is the spectacular scenery of the Taos area—the gorgeous sunsets, the deep blue sky, the big brooding mountains, the cheerful brimming creeks, the sagebrush meadows. This is some of the prettiest country in the Southwest, and the director took full advantage of it in making this film. Earlier in his life, Redford went to Paris and studied to be a painter—one can see that part of his experience throughout this film, in its careful attention to landscape. Much of *The Milagro Beanfield War* was shot in the small village of Truchas, which is located on the Old High Road to Taos (follow U.S. 285 north from Santa Fe for about 24 miles; turn east on State Route 76 and drive another 20 miles to Truchas). Additional footage was also shot in and around Taos (about 70 miles north of Santa Fe, via U.S. 285 and State Route 68), in the Santa Fe National Forest and in the Los Alamos area (Los Alamos is about 40 miles northwest of Santa Fe, via U.S. 285 and State Route 4).

Hispanic activist with a Thoreau-like streak of individualism (Joe Mondragon) and James Gammon, who is cast as the avaricious Anglo real estate developer (Ladd Devine) out to develop the "Miracle Valley Recreation Area." The film, which has become something of a cult classic since its release, follows the novel fairly closely, especially with respect to Nichols' brilliant humor and satire.

Lonesome Dove

Lonesome Dove is a sprawling epic that covers the length and breadth of the historic West, from the overgrown cattail banks of the Rio Grande River to the wide open buffalo prairie of Montana. Based on Larry McMurtry's Pulitzer-prize winning novel (1985)—arguably his finest literary work—the movie tells the story of the enduring friendship between two Texas Rangers: Augustus McCrae (Robert Duvall) and Captain W. F. Call (Tommy Lee Jones). When we first meet our two heroes they are the proprietors of the Hat Creek Cattle Company near Lonesome Dove, Texas. The two Rangers, and the various cowboys in their employ, are surviving, but only barely (we are told their ranch house has no roof, but "fortunately it only rained in Lonesome Dove once or twice a year"). Augustus, or Gus, is the leader of the two. As a character he bears a resemblance to Sam the Lion in McMurtry's earlier *The Last Picture Show* (played by Ben Johnson in the film; see Texas chapter). Gus has an unlikely dream—to move the half-wild Hat Creek longhorn herd a thousand miles north to Montana, where the grass is stirrup-deep and the land belongs to no one (sort of). Captain Call plays the laconic, skeptical foil to the garrulous, visionary Gus, but eventually he is persuaded to join his lifelong friend on this grand adventure into the unknown.

If the movie is about the relationship between two men, it is also the story of their lost frontier world—the women they loved (most notably Clara), the friends they held dear (Pea Eye, Deets, young Newt, old Bolivar the Cook), the enemies they fought (especially Blue Duck), the lands they crossed (deserts, mountains, rivers, all manner of badlands), and the often unusual people they met on their long journey. *Lonesome Dove* includes particularly strong performances by Tommy Lee Jones, Robert Duvall, and Angelica Huston (daughter of screen legend John Huston). Many critics believed that Duvall held the production, and the film narrative, together with his riveting performance of Gus. Throughout the film (which was a CBS television miniseries) the landscape plays an essential role, often rising to the level of becoming an active character in the story. It is a country—the Southwest—as big and tough, as kind and as cruel, as beautiful and sometimes as barren, as the people who live upon it. All of this was captured in the film, just as McMurtry had faithfully rendered it in the novel. *Lonesome Dove* remains one of the most highly rated television productions ever made, and has entered a permanent second life in video and cable release.

Lonesome Dove was filmed partly in southwestern Texas (see Texas chapter), but was shot primarily in New Mexico. Locations in northern New Mexico included the Santo Domingo Pueblo (take exit 252 on I-25, midway between Albuquerque and Santa Fe) and the San Ildefonso Pueblo (about 20 miles northwest of Santa Fe on State Route 502), as well as the Cook Ranch / Silverado Set and the Bonanza Creek Ranch (both of the latter are private movie filming sets in the Santa Fe area).

Lonely Are the Brave

Many years ago, before his stroke, the actor Kirk Douglas appeared on David Letterman's late-night interview program and was asked "Which film of all those you've made was your favorite?" Douglas did not hesitate. "That's simple," he replied, "*Lonely Are the Brave*." Letterman asked why. "Best script I ever worked from, best character I ever played." That's quite a statement, coming from an actor who performed in such classics as *Lust for Life* (1956), *Gunfight at the O.K. Corral* (1957), *Spartacus* (1960), and *Seven Days in May* (1964). It says a lot, though, about this moving and underrated modern Western, which was based on the fine novel by Edward Abbey (*The Brave Cowboy*, 1956). Directed by David Miller, with a screenplay by Oscar-winner Dalton Trumbo, *Lonely Are the Brave* includes performances by two actors who would eventually win Oscars—George Kennedy, for *Cool Hand Luke* (1967), and Walter Matthau, for *The Fortune Cookie* (1966)—as well as several actors who would become well known in television during the sixties and seventies: Bill Bixby *(The Incredible Hulk)*, William Schallert (affable, avuncular character player in numerous programs), and Carroll O'Connor *(All in the Family, In the Heat of the Night)*.

When we first meet cowboy Jack Burns (played by Kirk Douglas) he is resting beside his palomino mare "Whiskey" on the open range

Danny Glover (Joshua Deets), Ricky Schroeder (Newt Robbs), and Robert Duvall (Gus McCrae) in Simon Wincer's hit television mini-series LONESOME DOVE *(Astra Cinema, 1989). Courtesy Photofest.*

Kirk Douglas as Jack Burns finds freedom on his horse overlooking the Rio Grande and the encroaching Albuquerque in David Miller's LONELY ARE THE BRAVE *(Universal-International, 1962). Courtesy Eddie Brandt's Saturday Matinee.*

east of Albuquerque, New Mexico. He has ridden out of the nearby Sandia Mountains and is en route to town to visit his friend Paul Bonti (played by Michael Kane). Almost immediately the central conflict of the film is established, as Douglas takes note of the many signs of civilization—the high contrails of a B-52 bomber escorted by two jet fighters, the nearby telephone poles and utility towers, the barbed wire fence put up by the local Duke City (Albuquerque) Water and Power Commission. He commits his first act of civil disobedience by cutting the wire fence and crossing the boundary between the two worlds: the world of wild nature and the world of human nature. For the rest of the film he will represent the independent spirit of the wilderness in conflict with the forces of civilization.

Douglas is, we soon learn, a living dinosaur, almost reflexively at odds with the many rules and regulations of society. His historical antecedents are figures like Jim Bridger, who lived in the mountains beyond the pale of civilization, and Lonesome Bill Reynolds, who died beside Custer at Last Stand Hill, and hundreds of other men, and women, who lived on the Western frontier while it was still a frontier, and who loved its absolute freedom, even with all the risks. Inevitably, in this film, Douglas finds himself being pursued by the law for a minor transgression. The sheriff (played by Walter Matthau) has a sort of begrudging admiration for Douglas, but realizes, too, that he has a job to do. Eventually Douglas is driven, like some hunted animal, into the highest peaks of the Sandia Mountains, and there the story finally ends. Author Edward Abbey killed the Douglas character off in the novel. The movie leaves a more ambiguous ending.

Lonely Are the Brave was shot in and around Albuquerque. The initial sequence was shot near the present-day airport (take State Route 556 northeast of town). The north end of the Sandia Mountains is plainly visible a few miles to the east. The chase scene, which occupies much of the latter half of the film, and the climax, were shot in Tijeras Canyon east of town (once traversed by Route 66; now occupied by Interstate 40).

SOUTHERN NEW MEXICO

Although most filming is done in northern New Mexico, the landscapes in the southern part of the state (south of Albuquerque and Interstate 40) have been featured in several important films. Generally, the state becomes progressively drier in the south, as the semidesert grasslands are left behind and the Chihuahuan Desert (largest desert in North America) begins to take over. The southern part of the state includes several mountain ranges and three river systems (Pecos, Rio Grande, and Gila). In the Mogollon Mountains to the west is the one-thousand-square-mile Gila Wilderness, an area often referred to as the Yellowstone of the Southwest. Historically, the southern part of the state is known for the Coronado Expedition, which explored the area a quarter of a century before Shakespeare was born (1540); the Apache

John Nichols

John Nichols (born 1940) grew up in the east and later graduated from Hamilton College in New York (1962). After a year of teaching English in Barcelona, Spain, and another year of bohemian life in post–Beat Generation New York City, Nichols sold his first work of fiction, *The Sterile Cuckoo*. The novel explores the nuances of first love. In 1969, Alan Pakula, in his directorial debut, produced a film adaptation of the novel, starring Liza Minnelli (daughter of Judy Garland). The film was a critical and commercial success and shortly thereafter Nichols moved to Taos, New Mexico, where he has lived ever since.

Taos has proven to be the perfect residence for Nichols. The ancestral home of Pueblo Indians and, more recently, of such historical figures as Kit Carson and Jim Bridger, Taos has long served as one of the major art centers in the Southwest. The dramatic scenery has inspired, among others, such master oil painters as Ernest Blumenschein and Joseph Sharp. In such a fertile aesthetic milieu, Nichols has found an ideal creative habitat. Early on, Nichols became involved in the cultural and class struggles of northern New Mexico, where Indian and Hispanic activists are often involved in battles to preserve indigenous values. From these experiences Nichols developed the idea for *The Milagro Beanfield War*, which was made into the film by director Robert Redford in 1986. With two more novels in the trilogy, viewers may yet see another Southwestern film emerge from Nichols' unique body of work.

Author John Nichols is best known for his novels THE STERILE CUCKOO *and* THE MILAGRO BEANFIELD WAR, *which were made into films. Courtesy John Nichols.*

Wars (Geronimo was born and raised on the upper Gila River); the Lincoln County Wars (Billy the Kid is buried near Fort Sumner); the Trinity Site (where the first atomic bomb was detonated in 1945); and the White Sands Missile Range (an alternative landing site for the Space Shuttle).

Films made in the southern part of the state include *King Solomon's Mines* (filmed in both White Sands National Monument and Carlsbad Caverns, 1950); *The Tall Texan* (filmed in Deming and City of Rocks State Park, 1953); *The Salt of the Earth* (filmed in and around Silver City, 1954); *Hang 'Em High* (see below); *Bite the Bullet* (filmed in White Sands National Monument, 1975); *The Man Who Fell to Earth* (filmed in White Sands National Monument, 1976); and, more recently *Young Guns II* (filmed in White Sands National Monument, 1990), and *White Sands* (filmed in White Sands National Monument, 1992).

Hang 'Em High

Hang 'Em High was filmed in 1967, shortly after Clint Eastwood returned to the United States following his successful spaghetti-Western period (1964–1966). In a recent interview Clint Eastwood said that what attracted him most to *Hang 'Em High* (released in 1968) was the ambiguous treatment of the issue of capital punishment. In the film Clint Eastwood plays Jed Cooper, a small-time cattle rancher who is falsely accused of stealing cattle and who survives his own lynching. He then seeks revenge on the group of men, who, in a mistaken rush to judgment, hanged him from a cottonwood tree along the Rio Grande River. For the production, thirty-eight-year-old Eastwood surrounded himself with an impressive cast of actors, including Inger Stevens (well known at the time for her television series *The Farmer's Daughter*), Ben Johnson (three years later he received an Oscar for his performance in *The Last Picture Show*), Dennis Hopper (he directed and starred in the Oscar-winning *Easy Rider* one year later), Bruce Dern (he went on to perform a lead role in the Oscar-winning *Coming Home* in 1978), Pat

Hingle (a seasoned character actor who often appears in Eastwood pictures, such as *The Gauntlet* in 1977, and film veteran Bob Steele [*Of Mice and Men* (1940), *The Enforcer* (1951), *Rio Bravo* (1959), *The Comancheros* (1961)].

Shortly after being hung, Eastwood is cut down and saved by the local sheriff (Ben Johnson), with the following line: "Some people may call this hell, but you're still in Oklahoma Territory." Eastwood is then taken to town and held for a time in general lockup. Eventually, once the facts are sorted out, he is released by the territorial judge (played flawlessly by the gritty, no-nonsense Pat Hingle). By that time, Eastwood's herd has been run off and he has no horse or saddle. To make amends, Hingle offers Eastwood an interesting opportunity— become a federal marshal, track down those responsible for the hanging, and bring them in for trial. In this capacity, Eastwood then hunts the gang down, one by one, until he finally reaches the powerful rancher at the center of the injustice (played by Ed Begley, Sr., who had in 1962 won an Oscar for his portrayal of Boss Finley in *Sweet Bird of Youth;* his son is Ed Begley, Jr., once a doctor on the television show *St. Elsewhere* and now a regular guest on Jay Leno's *Tonight Show*). *Hang 'Em High* also has a romantic subplot involving Eastwood and Inger Stevens, who portrays a widow looking for the killer of her husband (also Begley, Sr.).

Both *Hang 'Em High* and *Bonnie and Clyde* were much-criticized at the time of their release for their violence, but they seem rather innocent and mild compared to cinema today (as in *Pulp Fiction*). Art reflects its times and the late 1960s were a violent period—political assassinations, urban and campus riots, the My Lai Massacre in Vietnam. Both films were simply holding a mirror up to their society. Made for a budget of less than two million dollars, *Hang 'Em High* grossed nearly twenty million dollars. The surprising success of the film made it increasingly easier for Eastwood to get the studio backing necessary for him to follow his creative instincts.

OPPOSITE: *Clint Eastwood as lawman Jed Cooper fights Ed Begley, Sr. as Wilson in Ted Post's* HANG 'EM HIGH *(UA, 1967). Courtesy Eddie Brandt's Saturday Matinee.*

Hang 'Em High was shot in the Chihuahuan desert around Las Cruces. As in many Southwestern films, it used the desert as a metaphor for the bleakness of its message, which underscored the impossibility of achieving justice through mob-rule and blind retribution. The opening sequence was shot just north of Las Cruces near the town of Dona Ana along the Rio Grande River. The San Andreas and Organ Mountains can be clearly seen to the east. The sand dune sequence was shot in White Sands National Monument (about 60 miles northeast of Las Cruces via U.S. 70).

OTHER LOCATIONS IN NEW MEXICO

CUMBRES & TOLTEC SCENIC RAILROAD (Chama station is located about 100 miles north of Santa Fe on U.S. 84)—The opening scene for *Indiana Jones and the Last Crusade* (1989) was shot on this scenic narrow gauge, as were scenes for more recent films such as *Wyatt Earp* (with Kevin Costner, Gene Hackman, Dennis Quaid, and Isabella Rossellini, 1994).

TAOS (located about 70 miles north of Santa Fe, via U.S. 285 and State Route 68)—Taos pueblo, on the north side of town, is one of the most filmed spots in the area, as in *Hollywood or Bust* (with Dean Martin and Jerry Lewis, 1956) and, more significantly, *Easy Rider* (1969). This is the tallest pueblo in the Southwest and one of the oldest. Some parts of it have been in continuous occupation for a thousand years. In the film *Natural Born Killers* (1994), outlaws Woody Harrelson and Juliette Lewis perform their marriage ritual on the bridge over the Taos Gorge west of town (on U.S. 64). The bridge is one of the highest in the country (650 feet above the river). The D. H. Lawrence ranch north of Taos was featured in *Easy Rider* (drive about 15 miles north on State Route 522 to the Kiowa Ranch turn-off, follow 5 miles east). Another feature of interest in Taos is the Kit Carson Home and Museum (half a block east of the Taos Plaza on Kit Carson Road).

GHOST RANCH (located about 14 miles northwest of Abiquiu on U.S. 84)—This area in the beautiful Rio Chama Basin has been used for many films, including *The Light That Failed* (with Walter Huston, 1939), *Showdown* (with Dean Martin, Rock Hudson, and Ed Begley, Jr., 1973), *The Groove Tube* (with Chevy Chase, 1974), *City Slickers* (with Billy Crystal and Jack Palance, 1991), and *Wyatt Earp* (1994).

SANTA FE (located about 60 miles north of Albuquerque on Interstate 25)—The Santa Fe Plaza, located in the heart of the historic part of town, has been featured in several films, most notably *Twins* (1989), with Danny DeVito and Arnold Schwarzenegger. The Palace of

Lawrence Kasdan's WYATT EARP *(Warner Bros., 1994) is a modern remake of the famous gunfight at the OK Corral with Kevin Kostner as Wyatt Earp. Courtesy Eddie Brandt's Saturday Matinee.*

Edward Abbey

Edward Abbey was born in 1928 and raised in the Allegheny Mountains of Pennsylvania. After two years of Army service in post-War Europe, he attended the University of New Mexico, graduating in 1951 with a degree in philosophy. In September of 1953 Abbey entered the graduate philosophy program at Yale, but left after two weeks, homesick for the West. Three years later he received an M.A. in philosophy from the University of New Mexico, writing a thesis entitled "Anarchism and the Morality of Violence" (a subject which by its nature precluded, probably intentionally, any further academic career). Abbey also briefly attended Wallace Stegner's renowned writing workshop at Stanford University, leaving after a year to work as a fire lookout in the Apache National Forest (Arizona).

Abbey's first novel, *Jonathan Troy* (1954), came and went without notice, but his second novel, *The Brave Cowboy* (1956), established him as a storyteller of unusual talent. Throughout the fifties, as his writing career slowly took shape, Abbey worked as a seasonal park ranger, most notably at Arches National Monument (*Desert Solitaire*, 1968), and as a seasonal fire lookout in various Southwestern national forests. In 1962 the cinematic version of *The Brave Cowboy*, entitled *Lonely Are the Brave*, was filmed in and around Albuquerque. Abbey's 1962 novel *Fire on the Mountain*, which tells the story of a cattle rancher forced from his desert spread by the federal government, was made into a 1981 television movie starring Buddy Epsen and Ron Howard (same title). The story is based on an incident that occurred during the 1940s, when the White Sands Missile Range was established in south-central New Mexico and the government seized several private ranches by right of eminent domain. In recent years Dennis Hopper has optioned Edward Abbey's environmental novel *The Monkey Wrench Gang* (1975), and it seems likely that at least one more film will be made from the author's considerable body of fiction.

The late Edward Abbey's philosophical and environmental literary works continue to attract readers despite his death. Courtesy Jack Dykinga.

Located in the small town of Truchas between Taos and Santa Fe, this traditional adobe church was used in THE MILAGRO BEANFIELD WAR *(Universal, 1987). Courtesy John Murray.*

the Governors, on the north side of the Plaza, is a massive adobe structure with thick walls. Built in 1610 (Shakespeare had six more years to live), it was the center of Spanish and then Mexican government until 1908, when the U.S. took over. Another area of interest is the Randall Davey Audubon Center (1800 Canyon Road), which was used for the art colony in *Twins* (1989).

LAS VEGAS (located about 70 miles east of Santa Fe on Interstate 25)—Originally a stop on the Santa Fe Trail, Las Vegas later became known as one of the rowdiest towns on the frontier, with visitors such as Billy the Kid and Doc Holliday. Las Vegas has hundreds of buildings listed on the National Register of Historic Places, particularly those that represent the Victorian period. The core of the town consists of some adobe structures in the downtown plaza. Las Vegas and the area around it have long been used in film (beginning in the silent era). Many of the old Tom Mix films were shot in Las Vegas. More recently, Las Vegas and its environs have appeared in such films as *Easy Rider* (1969), *Speechless* (1994), *Natural Born Killers* (1994), *The Hi Lo Country* (1999), and *All the Pretty Horses* (2000).

ACOMA PUEBLO (located 12 miles south of the junction of Interstate 40 and State Route 23, west of Pueblo)—Acoma, or the Sky City, has been continuously inhabited since about 1150. Several films have been made at Acoma, including *Acoma* (1929), *Way Out West* (1930), and *Sundown* (1941).

NATIONAL RADIO ASTRONOMY OBSERVATORY (VERY LARGE ARRAY TELESCOPE) (located about 50 miles west of Socorro on U.S. 60)—The VLA is the most advanced radio telescope in the world, with twenty-seven antennae (each measuring nearly ninety feet in diameter) positioned along several railroad tracks in the high desert (Plains of San Agustin). The railroad tracks range from ten to twelve miles long. The VLA is used to produce detailed radio maps of the most distant parts of the universe, as well as to search for signs of intelligent life in the galaxy on various likely frequencies. The VLA was the site of the opening sequences of the film *Contact* (with Jodie Foster, 1996), based on the science fiction novel by Carl Sagan. In the film Jodie Foster portrays a radio astronomer who monitors an extraterrestrial transmission, deciphers the transmission, and then helps the government follow its instructions. The final scene of the film was shot just to the west of the VLA, at Canyon de Chelly National Monument (see Arizona chapter).

FORT SUMNER (located 46 miles south of Interstate 40 via U.S. 84)—The grave of Billy the Kid—the subject of more films than any other Southwestern outlaw—is located in Fort Sumner (drive 2 miles south on State Route 272; the grave is located on the east side of the road).

THE GILA WILDERNESS AREA (located about 30 miles north of Silver City on State Route 15)—The Chiricahua Apache leader Geronimo was born near the headwaters of the Gila River. This according to his autobiography, which he dictated orally to a journalist shortly before his death in 1909. The Gila is one of the most beautiful areas in the Southwest. Visitors will quickly understand why the Apache fought so hard to preserve their homeland.

LORDSBURG (exit 20 on Interstate 10)—The 1939 film *Stagecoach* (see Arizona chapter) was based on a story about the Butterfield-Overland stage route from Lordsburg west into southeastern Arizona (Fort Bowie on Apache Pass). This area was often subjected to depredations during the "Cochise Wars" of the 1860s, after some of Cochise's relatives were executed by a young lieutenant at Apache Pass. The Shakespeare Ghost Town is located 2 miles south of town on the road to Animas (State Route 464). Another important historical site in the area is the Stein's Railroad Ghost Town (exit 5 on Interstate 10).

SILVER CITY (located 40 miles north of Interstate 10, via the Lordsburg exit and State Route 90)—One of the little-known but best films made in New Mexico—*The Salt of the Earth* (1953)—was filmed in and around Silver City (especially the giant open pit copper mine east of town). The film was a serious drama about striking mineworkers and showed the natural landscapes of the Southwest as they have sometimes been ravaged by humankind.

SHIPROCK (distinctive volcanic pinnacle located about 10 miles south of the town of Shiprock on U.S. 666)—The last scene of John Ford's *My Darling Clementine* (1946) features Henry Fonda riding off across the desert toward Shiprock. The unique feature has also appeared in numerous other films.

TEXAS

Filming began in Texas almost as soon as it did in California. Had history developed differently, Texas, rather than California, might have evolved into the filming capital of the country. Probably the lack of public land in Texas (which translates into higher production costs) played more of a role in the rise of California than anything else. In the beginning, though, Texas was a hot and rising star. The records of the Texas Film Commission indicate, for example, that in 1910 forty-three silent films were shot in the San Antonio area by the Star Film Company, including *A Bad Night at the Bridge*, *In the Tall Grass Country*, *A Plucky American Girl*, *Speed Versus Death*, and *A Texas Joke*. Since then, over eight hundred feature films have been made in the state. Films are big business in Texas. In 1998, an average year, fifteen films were shot in Texas, as well as numerous TV series, pilots, movies, miniseries, specials, and documentaries, projects that collectively brought over $200 million into the state economy.

As the largest state in the Lower 48, Texas offers filmmakers a rich array of natural and urban landscapes. It stretches from the southern bayou country to the high Chihuahuan Desert, from the old antelope prairie around Amarillo to the rugged Chisos Mountains along the Mexican border. Its cities are renowned for the beauty of their architecture. As a cultural area, Texas is a place of myth and legend. Here the Texas Rangers were formed in 1826, and here they fought outlaws and Comanche raiders. Here the Battle of The Alamo took place in 1836, and here the historic cattle drives began. Here the oil barons found great wealth on the land, and here a young Georgia O'Keeffe discovered the quiet beauty of Palo Duro Canyon. Here the motorcade of President Kennedy turned a bright corner one dark afternoon, and here contemporary talents such as Larry McMurtry, Cormac McCarthy, Willie Nelson, and Waylon Jennings live and create.

The word "Texas" evokes a place on the map as well as a province of the imagination—a land where a diverse people continue to make important history. Part of the United States, yet once part of Mexico (and for a time a sovereign country), Texas remains a state with an independent spirit, a place whose greatest wealth is its people and whose landscapes are as inspiring as any in the Southwest.

WEST TEXAS

West Texas is a rugged, sunbaked country, a landscape of long dry vistas and distant purple mountains, prickly pear cactus pads and barbed yucca, howling coyotes and perpetual winds. The place-names evoke the singular nature of the place: a county seat named Hereford; a crossroads named Goodnight; a canyon with the Spanish name of Palo Duro; a mountain range named Apache; a tributary of the Pecos River

OPPOSITE: *The Chihuahuan Desert stretches throughout much of southwest Texas. Courtesy John Murray.*

named the Independence. Here is the land that gave the world the genius of Buddy Holly (born and raised in Lubbock) and the legend of Judge Roy Bean (near Langtry), as well as the indefatigable border rangers that inspired Larry McMurtry's two best-loved creations: Augustus McCrae and Captain Call. To this day, the Trans-Pecos region (a South Carolina–sized area south of the Pecos and north of the Rio Grande) remains one of the most isolated parts of the United States. Despite the fact that the world has entered the twenty-first century, there is, incredibly, still no town or settlement on the American side of the Rio Grande from Esperanza to Candelaria—a distance of over 120 miles.

If Texas has its version of Hollywood, it is this wild western part of the state, where dozens of major films have been made. Most filming has been concentrated in two areas: the mountainous region around historic Fort Davis and Alpine (about 200 miles southeast of El Paso via Interstate 10); and the lowlands around Del Rio (about 200 miles southeast of Alpine on U.S. 90), which includes Bracketville (made famous by John Wayne's 1962 production of *The Alamo*). One of the best films to come out of the first area was the Oscar-winning *Giant* (1956) which starred James Dean (in his final film), Elizabeth Taylor, Dennis Hopper, and Rock Hudson (in his best performance). The movie was shot on location at Marfa, a ranching community just south of Alpine. *Giant* told the story of two rival ranchers, played by Hudson and Dean, and the beautiful woman (Elizabeth Taylor) who came between them. It was recently listed by the American Film Institute as one of the one hundred best films of the twentieth century. Another area of note in west Texas is Claude, near Amarillo, where *Hud* was filmed in 1962 (Amarillo gained some national attention in 1998 when Oprah Winfrey was put on trial there for defaming the Texas cattle industry, a proceeding in which she prevailed).

Other important films shot wholly or in part in west Texas include *Geronimo* (with Gene Lockhart, 1939), which was shot in the El Paso area; *The Sundowners* (with Robert Preston and John Barrymore, Jr., 1950), which was shot in the Davis Mountain area; *Midnight Cowboy* (1968), which was shot around Big Spring about 100 miles south of Amarillo; *The Sugarland Express* (directorial debut of Steven Spielberg, with Ben Johnson and Goldie Hawn, 1973), which was shot around Del Rio; *Centennial* (the miniseries based on the James Michener novel), which was shot at the Alamo movie site at Brackettville and around Del Rio; *Lonesome Dove* (CBS miniseries, 1988), which was shot in the Del Rio area, including the Alamo movie site at Brackettville; *Courage Under Fire* (1995), which was shot at Fort Bliss near El Paso; and *Lone Star* (with Kris Kristofferson, 1995), which was shot at Eagle Pass and Del Rio.

In the end, west Texas is as unique a province of the Southwest as northern Arizona or southern California. It is a desert land where the highways go on forever and the dusty little towns look like something from a Marty Robbins country-western song, a place, as Larry McMurtry wrote in *Lonesome Dove*, where the "clouds [are] scarcer than cash money, and cash money [is] scarce enough."

Hud

Hud is based on Larry McMurtry's best-selling 1961 novel *Horseman, Pass By* (the title is from a William Butler Yeats poem: "Cast a cold eye/on life, on death,/ Horseman, pass by"). The film ignited the careers of Larry McMurtry and Paul Newman, both of whom would go on to become dominating forces in American cinema. *Hud* fell into a group of nontraditional Westerns in the early sixties—including *The Misfits* (1961) and *Lonely Are the Brave* (1962)—that sought to redefine the region, and the genre of the Western, in contemporary terms. The film, like the novel, focused on the relationships between three generations of Texans: a ranching patriarch past his prime, Homer Bannon (Melvyn Douglas); his rebellious son, Hud (Paul Newman); and his young nephew, Lonnie (Brandon De Wilde). Adding to the tension is the

OPPOSITE: *Paul Newman stars as the rebellious, womanizing Hud, in a scene with Melvyn Douglas (his father Homer Bannon), Brandon De Wilde (his brother Lon Bannon), and Yvette Vickers (Lily Peters) in Martin Ritt's dark drama* HUD *(Paramount, 1963). Courtesy Eddie Brandt's Saturday Matinee.*

John Wayne as Davy Crockett and Richard Widmark as Jim Bowie in John Wayne's THE ALAMO *(UA, 1960). Courtesy Eddie Brandt's Saturday Matinee.*

housekeeper/cook, an attractive woman named Halmea (Patricia Neal).

The plot focuses on an outbreak of hoof-and-mouth disease among the family cattle. Hud argues that the herd should be sold off as quickly possible. Homer, an uncompromising man of principle, refuses to pass the diseased livestock on to unsuspecting buyers, and instead orders the entire herd slaughtered. The conflict between the two men grows and eventually the elder Bannon succumbs to a heart attack. Hud then inherits the ranch, planning to drill for oil, and young Lonnie, disillusioned by what has transpired, leaves for a future elsewhere. Like *The Last Picture Show* (1971), which was also based on a McMurtry novel, *Hud* was filmed in black and white. This lends an abstract, nostalgic quality to the film, and quietly underscores the battle between good (Homer) and evil (Hud) at the core of the narrative. The story has all the darkness and power of a Eugene O'Neill family play, while never losing its bedrock fidelity to the landscapes and the people of the Southwest. The film received three Oscars: Best Supporting Actor (Melvyn Douglas), Best Actress (Patricia Neal), and Best Cinematography (James Wong Howe). Newman would eventually receive an Oscar in 1987 for his reprisal of the *The Hustler* character Fast Eddie Felson in *The Color of Money*.

Hud was filmed in and around Claude, Texas, which is located about 20 miles southeast of Amarillo on U.S. 287 in Armstrong County. This is the heart of the west Texas cattle country—tornadoes every spring and blizzards every winter, as well as endless stretches of old buffalo prairie interrupted by the occasional windmill or oil rig. Over it all, looms a vast chromium blue vault of Texas sky.

The Alamo

If *Hud* was a nontraditional Western, a black-and-white vignette of the new West, then John Wayne's three-hour epic *The Alamo*, shot in wide-angle Technicolor and elevating the massacre victims to the status of heroes, was a look backward at the Golden Age of the genre and of western history. Filmed in 1960 in south Texas, *The Alamo* was intended to be the crowning achievement of Wayne's career, a film on which

Rio Grande River. Courtesy John Murray.

he staked his personal fortune. In the end it cost over $11 million to make and generated around $7 million on initial release. More disappointing was the fact that the film garnered only one Oscar (Best Sound), after having been nominated in eleven categories, including Best Picture and Best Supporting Actor. For the rest of the decade Wayne would struggle, sometimes filming three or four pictures a year, to restore his crippled finances. Even worse, Wayne lost one lung to cancer not long after the film came out, a painful disability which he never let slow him down.

Today *The Alamo* remains one of the most important films ever to be filmed in Texas. The film is known both for the strength of its cast—which includes John Wayne, Richard Widmark, Richard Boone, and Laurence Harvey—as well as the technical success of several of its key sequences (most notably, the climactic scene). It provides as detailed an account as has ever been produced of the historic "creation myth" of Texas. The movie set (about 6 miles north of Brackettville on State

Route 674) remains a popular tourist site in the area, and is still actively used by film production companies (about two dozen times in the last decade). The site includes a full-scale replica of the Alamo and San Antonio as it existed in 1836.

North Texas

North Texas is a big country, ranging from the fertile valley of the Red River on the north to the fabled Texas Hill Country on the south. It includes densely populated areas—the burgeoning Dallas–Fort Worth metroplex—as well as regions that are as windswept and lonely as can be found anywhere on the southern prairie. North and West of Dallas is "McMurtry Country," the ranching outliers where the legendary novelist and screenwriter grew up. Dallas itself, like most major American cities, has seen quite a bit of filming over the years, both for the movies and for television (the long-running series *Dallas;* the popular *Walker, Texas Ranger*). Well-known films made in and around Dallas include *Bonnie and Clyde* (with Warren Beatty and Faye Dunaway, 1968), *Silkwood* (with Meryl Streep and Kurt Russell, 1982), and *JFK* (directed by Oliver Stone, 1991). *Bonnie and Clyde* was shot on location at several rural towns around Dallas, including Maypearl and Venus, near Waxahachie; and Rowlett, near Mesquite. At least one local bank used in the film was a bank that Bonnie and Clyde actually robbed—the abandoned 1930's-era bank is located in the small rural community of Pilot Point, about 17 miles northeast of Denton on U.S. 377.

The Last Picture Show

Hundreds of films are made every year, all with prayerful expectations and most at prodigious expense. Most quickly pass into oblivion. A dozen, sometimes only half a dozen, are fondly remembered. A very few (as in *Casablanca, An American in Paris,* or *A Streetcar Named Desire*) go on to become cult films, to be watched again and again, and to achieve classic status. Generally only one or two of these films come into being each year. Against all odds, Peter Bogdanovich's *The Last*

Picture Show (1971), based on Larry McMurtry's second novel, has achieved just that, and over the decades become a film that audiences and scholars perennially return to with admiration and affection. Its omission from the American Film Institute's list of the one hundred best movies of the twentieth century is puzzling (especially with the inclusion of several very good but not great films).

Set on the prairie south of the Red River, the Bogdanovich film, like the novel, tells the story of a community of Texans living in a dreary rural town. The mythical Thalia is a forgotten backwater in which dreams rarely come true and most people merely survive (in other words, what life is like for 99 percent of the human race). Shot in stark black and white, the film captures all the despair and emptiness of both the geographic and the human landscape. The cast included Jeff Bridges (as the strong but shallow high school fullback Duane), Timothy Bottoms (his quiet, brooding friend Sonny Crawford), Ben Johnson (as Sam the Lion, owner of the last movie theater and the local pool hall), Ellen Burstyn (as the wistful Mrs. Farrow, Sam's lover from long ago), twenty-one-year-old Cybill Shepherd (the former Miss Teenage Memphis as the ineffable Jacy Farrow), and Cloris Leachman (as the Madame Bovary–esque Ruth Popper, the football coach's wife). The film follows this unlikely cast of characters during a short but axial period in their lives—the coming of age of the younger generation, the closing of the movie theater and the death of Sam Lion (representing the spirit of the town), and Cloris Leachman's desperate reaching out for love with the high school student Timothy Bottoms. Both Ben Johnson and Cloris Leachman would receive Oscars for their performances.

The Last Picture Show was shot in Larry McMurtry's home town of Archer City, about 20 miles south of Wichita Falls on State Route 79. The still-vacant theater that inspired the film can be found at 115 East Main Street (many people drive up from Dallas–Forth Worth on the weekends to view the theater and tour the area). *Texasville* (1990), a lackluster follow-up to *The Last Picture Show* was also filmed in Archer City. In recent years Larry McMurtry has attempted to transform the struggling town into the used-bookstore capital of the world (seriously).

Timothy Bottoms as Sonny Crawford and Ben Johnson as Sam the Lion, who won an Oscar for Best Supporting Actor, witness the slow death of a small town in Peter Bogdanovich's THE LAST PICTURE SHOW *(Columbia, 1971). Courtesy of the Academy of Motion Picture Arts and Sciences.*

Robert Duvall

Robert Duvall is the chameleon of American cinema, an actor of legendary versatility, whether portraying the feeble-minded resident of a small town *(To Kill a Mockingbird)*, a cocky Marine Corps fighter pilot *(The Great Santini)*, or an anxiety-plagued southern revival minister *(The Apostle)*. The son of a Navy admiral, Duvall was born in San Diego in 1930. After graduating from Principia College in Illinois, Duvall served for two years in the military and then moved to New York, where he studied acting. By the time Duvall was in his early thirties, he had become a sought-after actor, well known for his careful attention to the small but significant details of behavior that can reveal character even more than dialogue and action.

Two films will forever bond the acting legacy of Robert Duvall to the landscapes of the American Southwest: *Tender Mercies* and *Lonesome Dove*. The first, shot on location in Waxahachie, Texas, employs the wide-open Texas prairie as a silent but essential character in the film. The second, *Lonesome Dove*, brilliantly captured the hardship and humor of the Old West.

Duvall remains one of the most active members of the film community. In 1998, Duvall's film *The Apostle*, which he wrote, financed, directed, and starred in, was awarded a Golden Globe. He received an Oscar nomination for his performance in the film. Like few other actors—one thinks of a handful of such venerable figures as Gary Cooper, John Wayne, and Clint Eastwood—Duvall has established an immortal legacy in Western film.

Robert Duvall as Mac Sledge, is an alcoholic, ex-singer in TENDER MERCIES *(Universal, 1983). Courtesy Photofest.*

Tender Mercies

Based on the brilliant screenplay by Horton Foote, *Tender Mercies* tells the story of a man (played by Robert Duvall) who loses everything and then, rather than surrendering to despair, somehow finds a way to keep going and make a new and better life for himself. Anyone who has ever stumbled off the path, and found themselves lost in a strange place (both geographically and spiritually), can relate to this beautiful and timeless story. When we first meet Mac Sledge (the Duvall character), the country-western star has been dumped drunk in the middle of the night at a lonely crossroads on the Texas prairie by his limousine-driving big city "friends." The next morning he walks into the motel office, admits to the owner, Rosa Lee (played by Tess Harper) that he is penniless, and offers to do odd jobs to pay for his room. Days turn into weeks turn into months. Sonny stays at the motel, sobers up, falls in love with the woman (a war widow with a ten-year-old son, Sonny), and makes a new life for himself. Change comes when he is recognized by a group of local musicians in a hardware store, is persuaded to record with them, and then becomes famous again (only to have the teenage daughter he had with his former wife, Dixie, also a country-western star, killed in a car accident). One of the little-known but amazing facts about *Tender Mercies* is that Duvall actually wrote all of the songs that he performs in the film. Duvall was awarded an Oscar in 1983 for his performance. Like so many north Texas films, *Tender Mercies* was shot on location in and around Waxahachie south of Dallas. The local chamber of commerce offers a map of specific sites used in the making of *Tender Mercies* and other Waxahachie films (write to the Chamber of Commerce, Waxahachie, Texas 75165).

SOUTH TEXAS

South Texas includes three historic cities—Austin, San Antonio, and Houston—as well as the picturesque Hill Country and the Lower Rio Grande Valley. The landscape is gentle and often rolling, the rivers broad and slow-moving. The bluebonnet wildflower displays each spring are the stuff of legend, the bass fishing in the summer months can be extraordinary, and every winter thousands in blaze orange flock to the region for its world-famous deer hunting. Many Texans believe this is the most beautiful part of their state. The history of south Texas is rich and includes the Alamo (located in San Antonio), the training grounds of Teddy Roosevelt's Rough Riders, and the birthplace of President Lyndon Baines Johnson. Austin, the state capital, is considered the intellectual and aesthetic heart of the state. Since the days of Hank Williams and Elvis Presley, Austin has been known as the music capital of Texas. South Texas also includes the legendary King Ranch, which at 1.2 million acres is roughly half the size of Rhode Island (it was the model for the ranch in the Oscar-winning film *Giant* in 1956).

In the early days of filming, the area in and around San Antonio was often used—over one hundred silents were shot in the region during the period from 1910 to 1930. Later the area became a center for talking films (the first sound Alamo picture was shot in San Antonio in 1936). More recently, a number of popular movies have been filmed in south Texas, including the original *Getaway* (with Steve McQueen and Ali McGraw; the film featured, among other places, the renowned "River Walk" part of San Antonio, 1972); *The Sugarland Express* (featuring Steven Spielberg's directorial debut; the film was shot in and around Houston, 1973); *Urban Cowboy* (see below, 1980); *The Best Little Whorehouse in Texas* (with Dolly Parton; the film was shot in and around Austin, 1982); *Terms of Endearment* (won four Oscars, including best acting for Jack Nicholson and Shirley MacClaine; the film was shot in and around Houston, 1985); *A Perfect World* (with Kevin Costner and Clint Eastwood; the film was shot in and around Austin, 1993); and *Selena* (with Jennifer Lopez; the film was shot in and around San Antonio and Corpus Christi, 1996).

Urban Cowboy

As the title suggests, this film deals with a ubiquitous paradox of the modern West—the cowboy who lives in the city. The two major characters, Bud (John Travolta) and Sissy (Debra Winger), are working hard

but still find themselves struggling on the margins of society, with barely enough money for "truck and trailer payments." They exist in a colorful, energetic, self-contained subculture of other "urban cowboys" who gather at a traditional Texas honky-tonk, or country-western dance club, called Gilley's. Bud works by day as a roughneck, or oil worker, on the oil fields that virtually surround Houston. Each night he comes to Gilley's to pit himself against a mechanical bull. The film looks at the myth of the American cowboy, which is central to the films of the American Southwest, through an unusual prism, which is the city. In this respect, it is somewhat similar to *Midnight Cowboy* (1969), filmed partly in west Texas, which also places the cowboy out of his element. The dream of the cowboy life—which is really a dream of self-reliance and independence—is the only thing that keeps the characters of *Urban Cowboy* alive, as they struggle to maintain their freedom and dignity in the dehumanizing world of urban wage-labor. This popular film came after Travolta's extraordinary success in *Grease* (1978), and helped to establish Debra Winger as an actress of unusual ability (she would later star in *Terms of Endearment,* also filmed in Houston). It is probably the only Western ever made that does not include at least one horse, or at least one shoot-out. *Urban Cowboy* was filmed in and around Pasadena, an eastern suburb of Houston. The original Gilley's Club (4500 Spencer) burned down in the early 1990s.

OTHER LOCATIONS IN TEXAS

SOUTHFORK RANCH (from Interstate 75 travel north to Parker Road, go east 6 miles, and turn right on FM 2551)—Daily tours are given of this location, which was the mythical home of the equally mythical Ewing family in the long-running (fourteen seasons) television program *Dallas* [a typical exchange between two of the master thespians in the cast—Bobby Ewing (played by Patrick Duffy, the youngest son):

John Travolta as Bud, a modern cowboy in an urban setting, dances with his mistress, Madolyn Smith-Osborne as Pam, in James Bridge's URBAN COWBOY *(Paramount, 1980). Courtesy Eddie Brandt's Saturday Matinee.*

"Daddy, you gave me the power to run Ewing Oil!" Jock Ewing (family patriarch): "Bobby, I didn't give you power. Power is what you take."

DEALEY PLAZA (lower downtown Dallas on Elm Street north of Reunion Park)—The Texas Schoolbook Depository Building, from which Lee Harvey Oswald fired the shots that killed President Kennedy on November 22, 1963, is now maintained as a historic site, with a small museum and guided tours of the sixth floor. Exhibits feature photographs, artifacts, and films. The depository is located on the northwest corner of Houston and Elm streets. The Dealey Plaza area was

OPPOSITE: *Robert Duvall as Mac Sledge shows Allan Hubbard, his stepson Sonny, what it was like when he was a big country music star in Bruce Beresford's* TENDER MERCIES *(Universal, 1983). Courtesy Eddie Brandt's Saturday Matinee.*

Linda Gray (Sue Ellen Ewing Lockwood), Larry Hagman (John Ross "J.R." Ewing), Barbara Bel Geddes (Ellie Ewing Farlow), Jim Davis (John Ross "Jock" Ewing, Sr.), Charlene Tilton (Lucy Ewing Cooper), Victoria Principal (Pamela Barnes Ewing), and Patrick Duffy (Bobby Ewing) in Dwight Adair and Barry Crane's popular television drama DALLAS *(Warner Bros., 1978–1991). Courtesy Photofest.*

used by Oliver Stone in 1991 when he was filming his controversial historical reconstruction *JFK*.

THE LBJ SPACE CENTER (located 25 miles southeast of Houston on Interstate 45)—If you liked Ron Howard's Oscar-winning film *Apollo 13* (1995), you'll love this unique facility. The museum features an entire *Saturn V* rocket—the ship that took the men to the moon—over on its side (each of the five main engine nozzles is large enough to drive a truck through). Inside the museum, you can reach out and touch one of the Apollo space ships that circled the moon (the honeycombed surface is still charred from re-entry), as well as view many other fascinating artifacts from space history (including a real moon rock under glass).

THE ALAMO (Alamo Plaza at Alamo and Houston Streets in downtown San Antonio)—The original stone mission became a last-stand fortress for James Bowie, Davy Crockett, and about 180 other freedom-fighters in 1836, and is the single most important historic site in Texas. The building, which has been restored and remodeled, includes a museum, library, and gift shop.

ALAMO VILLAGE (located about 30 miles east of Del Rio on U.S. 90)—This is it, the location that cost John Wayne millions of dollars to build in 1960 for his epic film *The Alamo*. The Western town and movie set is open year-round for visitors.

JUDGE ROY BEAN MUSEUM (1 mile west of Langtry on U.S. 90)—In 1882 Judge Roy Bean established himself as justice of the peace at this obscure location. Over the next few years he tried with some success to bring law and order to the vast wilderness north of the Rio Grande. His legendary exploits served as the basis for a film, *The Life and Times of Judge Roy Bean* (with John Huston as director and Paul Newman both in the starring role and as co-producer, 1972). The film was shot primarily in Arizona at the Old Tucson site (see Arizona chapter).

Larry McMurtry

Few authors have so dominated American cinema as Larry McMurtry. Born in Wichita Falls, Texas, in 1936, McMurtry graduated from North Texas State University and then went on to study creative writing at Stanford under the Pulitzer-prize winning novelist Wallace Stegner. McMurtry's first work of fiction *Horseman, Pass By,* was published in 1961, when he was only twenty-five. The novel—a grimly realistic picture of the contemporary West—was a precocious work. It immediately drew comparisons to the first work of Hemingway, *The Sun Also Rises,* which was also published when its creator was only twenty-five. Two years later the movie *Hud,* based on McMurtry's novel, was released.

McMurtry's third novel—*The Last Picture Show*—was, like *Horseman, Pass By,* based on his youthful experiences during the 1950s in Archer County, Texas. The film version of the novel (1971) suprised everyone with its success. McMurtry's career, and vision of life, reached its culmination in two very different novels, both of which were made into successful films. *Terms of Endearment,* which followed the relationship of a Texas mother and daughter over the years, became one of the most successful films of all time, winning five Oscars in 1983. *Lonesome Dove,* which received a Pulitzer Prize in 1986, explored the exploits of two Texas Rangers. The popular television adaptation appeared in 1989.

Over the last forty years Larry McMurtry has successfully withstood the distractions and temptations that have undone so many other American writers (particularly those associated with the film industry). At every stage of his career—and there have been four, marked by his four most successful books—McMurtry has exhibited the same qualities: a penetrating and honest vision of human life, a tireless work ethic, and a steadfast committment to truth and excellence. Whether writing about two best friends on the old Texas frontier or a mother and daughter in the suburbs of contemporary Houston, McMurtry has displayed an uncanny ability to create believable characters, realistic dialogue and naturalistic plots. Hollywood may never see another writer with his unique set of talents, and the Southwest may never again have such a devoted and loving chronicler.

Larry McMurtry's home state serves as a source of inspiration for the author. Courtesy Diana Ossana/ Simon & Schuster.

AFTERWORD

"How long do I have, doc?"
> —John Wayne (the aging gunfighter) to Jimmy Stewart (the town doctor) in *The Shootist* (a film shot in Carson City, Nevada, 1976)

In the months before her death my seventy-one-year-old mother, who had never been much of a film-goer, suddenly began spending a lot of time in the local movie theaters. As I recall (this was the spring of 1998) she saw, among others, *Ulee's Gold*, *As Good As It Gets*, and *The Apostle*. She liked them all, each of which contained at least one Oscar-nominated performance, but I think her favorite was *Ulee's Gold*. *Titanic* she refused to see because, she said jokingly, she already knew the ending. I see now that, approaching the end of her life, she instinctively sought the theaters as part of a search for meaning. In the darkness of the balcony and the luminous images on the screen she was looking not so much for entertainment and diversion—they were not as important anymore—as for faith and understanding. What was this thing that had just happened to her, this thing called life? What was to be made of this other event about to occur, which would lead to the opposite of life? Those films, as mirrors of life, provided her with a sort of clarity and comfort that no physician, no priest could. When hope dwindles and nature stymies reason, when suffering intrudes and science is confounded, there is art.

As I wrote these pages I kept a photograph of William S. Hart beside me on the desk. Although not well known anymore, Hart was the first popular star of western silent films (from 1914 to 1925). Because he had already worked a lifetime outdoors in the west before coming to film (he was 44 when he made his first picture), Hart intimately understood the region and insisted on complete fidelity to landscape and character. In this sense, he was the father of the genre, the one person, more than any other, who established a bedrock standard of realism in western cinema. The photograph is a still from his last film, *Tumbleweeds* (United Artists, 1925, rereleased in 1939), which he both produced and starred in. A seven-reel epic (over 7,000 feet of film), the movie dramatized that pivotal moment on the frontier when the cattle drives had ended and the landrushes began. Hart portrayed Don Carver, a good man in an often bad world, who tries, and succeeds, in carving out a dignified life for himself and his true love, Molly Lassiter (played by Barbara Bedford). I have at all times, in writing this book, tried to create a work whose accuracy and devotion to subject would be something that Hart (born, incredibly, in 1872), and all those who followed him, would approve of.

Southwestern film is a work-in-progress. This book is a report, as it were, on the first one hundred years. It has tried to tell the story of a wonderful landscape and some of the films that have been inspired by

OPPOSITE: *William S. Hart as Dan Carver in King Baggot's* TUMBLEWEEDS *(UA, 1925). Courtesy Photofest.*

its deserts and mountains, men and women, storms and skies. Accomplished as the films are that have been created to date, the best, we can be certain, is yet to come. Fifty years from now, one hundred years from now, books like this will be written by people just like me. Actors and actresses who will not be born for another twenty years, directors still in daycare, cinematographers still on formula, will produce new classics. Some of these films will be based on the old Southwestern myths and legends—Geronimo and Cochise, Wyatt Earp and Billy the Kid, the Butterfield-Overland stage, the historic cattle drives, the gold mining boom towns. Others will be fresh stories on the oldest themes—the beauty of courage, the corrupting influence of power, alienation and loneliness, the centrality of love, the constancy of change, the resilience of the spirit, the force of a dream.

In the end it comes to this. When a deer is shot, it will retreat to the quietest, darkest place on the mountain. So, too, do we, in pain or fatigue, despair or distraction, seek out the refuge of the theater. There we are transported into another place for awhile, a landscape partly of this world and partly of the imagination. When we return to this realm we are changed, sometimes forever. We have seen a sky as blue as lapis lazuli, a green valley that goes on for a hundred miles, a man or a woman with a heart made of iron, or clay, or fire, or decayed wood, or the gentle radiance that comes from the stars. Even now, in a theater somewhere in the world, the house lights are going down and the tired faces of the audience are looking up, brightened by the moving images on the screen.

APPENDIX

GLOSSARY OF TERMS AND TITLES

Courtesy of Glen Canyon National Recreation Area

This is not a complete list of people on the film set. There are also people who, for example, build the sets, paint the scenes, work with the horses, drive the vehicles, maintain accounts, attend to correspondence and other secretarial duties, choreograph, coach dialogue, or advise in some other technical or special capacity (to name just a few).

ART DIRECTOR: The person responsible for designing all of the sets used in a motion picture.

ASSISTANT CAMERA OPERATORS: The people assisting with the camera, working directly for the cameraman. Duties include physical movement and setup of the camera, loading its magazines, cleaning the camera and its components. The first assistant is also called a "focus puller" and follows focus on the camera while actually filming.

ASSISTANT DIRECTORS (AD): The first AD is the right arm of the director, both in organizing the production and running the set. The second AD is responsible for the call sheets, movements of extras, and basically making certain that everything is in the right place at the right time.

ASSOCIATE PRODUCER: Represents the producer's interest when the producer is not personally on the production scene. He or she may control finances during the location shooting. For a commercial, the associate producer may be the set contact.

BOOM OPERATOR: Sound person who positions the microphone, trying to keep it as close to the speaker as possible without getting it into the picture, or without casting a shadow that can be seen in the picture. The mike is actually mounted on the end of a fish pole or boom.

CAMERAMAN OR CAMERA OPERATOR: The member of the crew who actually runs and maneuvers the camera.

CLAPPER (OR SLATE OR MARK): This person holds the clapboard or slate in front of the scene at the beginning of each shot. In a sound production, the clapper (or slate or mark) announces the scene number and brings the hinged portion of the clapper onto the slate with a sharp sound. This sound is synchronized later with the picture.

CRAFT SERVICES: Often provide assistance in keeping the set clean, providing coffee and snacks between meals, and other services that support the crew but are not related to actual filming operation.

DIRECTOR: Formulates and is responsible for the execution of the story requirements as set forth by the producer. Directs the efforts of the talent, the cameraman, the editor, and the lab, plus all the rest of the production company. In features, the director has artistic control. In episodic television, the producer holds artistic control, hiring different directors for individual episodes. In commercials, the director must work within the framework of the storyboard created by the advertising agency.

DIRECTOR OF PHOTOGRAPHY (DP): The person responsible for lighting the scene and setting up the shots. The members of the camera crew report to this position.

ELECTRICIAN: Technician responsible for connecting lights to the proper power supplies. He/she receives instructions from the gaffer and the cameraman or the Director of Photography.

EXTRAS: People who are seen in the filmed sequences of the picture, but in very minor roles without assigned lines of dialogue. They are directed by the assistant director and not the director.

GAFFER (ALSO CHIEF JUICER OR BOSS ELECTRICIAN OR CHIEF ELECTRICIAN): This is a lighting electrician who is in charge of the lighting crew or juicers. He/she reports to the cameraman or director of photography.

GREENSMAN: A set dresser specializing in organic materials such as trees, bushes, and flowers.

GRIPS: Manual laborer possessing special skills germane to film production. Just about everything that is lifted or moved or built on a set is done by grips. They load and unload equipment, build camera platforms, dig holes for camera placement, push the dolly, and move the set walls.

LOCATION MANAGER: The person responsible for finding, selecting, and finalizing the locations needed for the script. Responsible for obtaining permits, traffic control, parking. Is also the liaison for the company to neighbors and monitor of clean up. Works for the production manager.

LOCATION SCOUT: Independent contractor hired by a company to photograph potential locations and provide contact information to the company. Has no authority to make commitments for the company.

LEAD: (1) The principle actor or character in a picture such as the hero or heroine. (2) The person in charge of a small group of technicians on a special detail.

PRODUCER: The producer can be an individual that provides financing for and the supervision of the production of motion pictures or television. The final authority for all matters relating to how funds are spent.

PRODUCTION ASSISTANT (PA): A person working for the production manager, handling a variety of tasks. May be assigned to non-skilled tasks on the set such as preventing people from walking through a shot or picking up litter. Frequently an entry level position.

PRODUCTION MANAGER: In commercials, the executive in charge of all production arrangements, i.e., location contacts, negotiations, and shooting schedules. Authorizes payment of bills.

PROPERTY MAN: Person responsible for all the objects on the set that are handled by the cast.

PROPERTY MASTER: Property man and certified/licensed controller of all weapons.

RECORDIST (SOUND): Person in charge of operating the sound recorder. Places the mike, strings cable, and sets the controls of the recording equipment.

SCRIPT SUPERVISOR (CONTINUITY): Technician who times the actual filming and keeps notes on each scene and take to insure continuity of action and provides the vital information for editors.

SET DECORATOR: Person responsible for furnishings and draperies to create the appropriate ambiance on the set.

SET DRESSER: Technician working for the Set Decorator. Places furnishings, hangs draperies, and arranges objects used to dress the set (not handled by the cast).

SOUND ENGINEER: The technician responsible for the operation and maintenance of the sound equipment.

STUNT COORDINATOR: Person who plans and supervises those who execute activities involving an element of risk. Arranges for safety relating to stunts and choreographs the action. Acts as an advisor to the director.

TALENT: The performers in front of the camera.

TRANSPORTATION COORDINATOR: Supervises the transportation captain and Teamsters and manages all vehicles, parking, portable toilets, and removal of trash.

UNIT PRODUCTION MANAGER (UPM): One who handles much of the business associated with film or television production and makes arrangements for food, lodging, transportation, location work. He keeps budget and expenditure records, authorizes payment of bills.

TERMS AND ITEMS ASSOCIATED WITH FILMING ON LOCATION
Courtesy of Glen Canyon National Recreation Area

ANGLE OF VIEW: The amount of a scene that is take in by the lens, usually expressed in degrees.

APPLE BOX: Wooden box in one of three basic sizes (full, half, and quarter) used on the set in a variety of ways—to raise actors, furniture, lights, etc.

BASE CAMP: Staging area for equipment and large vehicles when filming in a variety of locations, or when parking adjacent to the filming location is not possible. Base camp can also be the site of activities not directly related to filming such as dressing and meals.

BLACKOUT CLOTH: Heavy, densely woven cloth used to cover windows and doors to facilitate day-for-night filming.

BOOM MIKE: Sound dolly with a long extendible boom enabling the operator to position the microphone and move it silently around the set following the actors.

BUTTERFLY: Net that can be stretched over an outdoor scene to soften sunlight.

CAMERA CAR: Vehicle that is outfitted to accommodate camera equipment and key personnel, for filming sequences on the road. Can also be used to tow vehicle being filmed.

CAMERA LEFT: The left side of the camera as the cameraman stands looking toward the action to be photographed. Camera right means the right side of the camera as the cameraman looks toward the action.

CENTURY STAND (ALSO C STAND): A metal stand for positioning a lighting accessory such as a flag, cookie, scrim, etc.

CINEMOBILE: A large, self-contained equipment truck.

CLAPPER (SEE ALSO SLATE): Two short boards hinged together and painted in a matching design. When sharply closed, they provide an audible and visual cue that is recorded simultaneously on film and sound tape. This helps to synchronize the film and sound during editing. A slate with relevant information, such as the scene and take number, is usually attached to the clapperboard.

COOKIE (ALSO CALLED KUKALORIS OR CUCALORIS): An irregularly perforated shadow-forming flag, opaque or translucent, made of plywood, plastic, etc. Used to create shadow textures.

CRAB DOLLY: Camera perambulator that eliminates the use of metal tracks and permits the camera to be moved in any horizontal direction. Vertical movement is approximately five feet.

CRANE: A large camera-mounting vehicle with a rotating and high rising arm, operated electrically or manually.

CREDIT LINE: The acknowledgments at the end of a film listing the cast, crew, and other production information including the locations used.

DAILIES (ALSO CALLED RUSHES): The first print from original footage, with or without synchronized sound tracks, delivered from the lab daily during the shooting period, for viewing by the director, cameraman, etc. If possible, sets are not struck until dailies have been viewed.

DAY FOR NIGHT: Shooting film in the daytime, in such a manner (lens filters, shading) that it gives the illusion of night.

DOLLY: A wheeled vehicle for mounting a camera and accommodating a camera operator and assistant. Often equipped with a boom on which the camera is mounted.

DOLLY TRACK: Parallel metal tracks laid on the ground to allow a dolly to move smoothly over rough or uneven surface or ground.

EDITORIAL: Still photography involving models or products that are intended to accompany articles in a magazine, rather than print advertisement.

ENG Crew (Electronic News Gathering): A small team, usually of fewer than five people, with a self-contained vehicle equipped with videotape, editing, and broadcast capability. Usually associated with daily news broadcasts.

Establishing Shot (also Master Shot): A shot, usually close to the beginning of a scene, that establishes the components of the scene in the viewer's mind.

Exterior: Any scene shot out of doors.

Fill Light: The light that is used to fill in shadowed areas, allowing for detail to be seen in those areas.

First Unit: Principle people on the set, including the director and actors, for filming dialogue and other scenes requiring the actors.

Fishpole: A long, lightweight, hand-held rod on which a microphone can be mounted in situations where the boom is not practical.

Flag: Shadow-casting device made of plywood, or cloth stretched on a metal frame. Specific types of flags include cutter, finger, gobo, and target.

Flat: A section of a studio set, usually modular, eight to ten feet high and six inches to twelve feet wide. Constructed of materials such as plywood, fireproof hessian, etc. Surface treatment varies from paints to wallpapers, papier-mâché, fabric, metals, etc.

Follow Shot: A shot in which the camera is moved to follow the action.

FX or EFX: Abbreviation for "effects" such as sound effects or special visual effects.

Gaffer's Tape: Wide adhesive tape used for securing lighting instruments, stands, cable, etc. on the set. Highly desirable by the crew, but often discarded as litter.

Greens: Plant material used in dressing the sets or landscapes.

Gobo: A black wooden, metal, or cloth screen used on a stand or a clamp to protect the lens from strong light which could cause a flare in the lens. (Sometimes called a "cookie.")

Golden Light: Term referring to the warm light that naturally occurs shortly before and after sunset or sunrise.

Hero: Term used in commercials to refer to camera-ready version of the product being advertised.

Hold: Term referring to a work day in which a production company has permission to be in a location, but not to schedule any activity to occur.

Honey Wagon: Jargon for portable dressing rooms with bathroom facilities.

IMO: Camera positioned in such a way as to isolate motion during an action sequence. Often the camera is set at a high speed to slow down the action. During filming, the camera is unattended and often the action occurs close to the camera itself.

Insert: A shot added to explain the action; e.g., a close-up of a letter, newspaper headline, gun, etc.

ITC: Intermittent traffic control. Involves holding traffic on a road in one or both directions for a period of time, generally not to exceed three minutes, for filming.

Location: Any place away from the studio used as a background for filming.

MOS: Filming without sound. Humorous coinage from the early days of cinema when immigrant German technicians spoke of shooting "mit [with] out sound."

Muscolight: Brand name for a large truck with a telescoping arm which supports an array of powerful lights, intended to illuminate a large area.

Night for Day: Shooting during darkness, while simulating daylight.

Pan: Pivotal camera movement in a horizontal plane. Sometimes used when describing pivotal camera movement in other planes.

Parallels: Metal scaffolding erected to provide elevated camera or lighting position.

PERMIT SERVICE: An independent agent hired by a production company to complete permitting requirements including application, payment, and pickup of required permits and business licenses, and notification of police and fire departments.

PICTURE CAR: Any vehicle to be used in front of the camera.

POV (POINT OF VIEW): Usually the camera position that simulates a view as seen by the actor.

POST PRODUCTION: All the processes that occur after the film has been shot and developed. Editing, titling, and mixing are all facets of post production.

PREP DAY: Work day preceding filming. Can include set construction or dressing, or rigging for stunts or special effects.

PROPS (PROPERTIES): Moveable objects on the set normally handled by actors.

REVERSE: What is seen opposite the location or set being shot; shot taken of what is behind the camera, or immediately adjacent to it in the establishing shot.

RUN-BY: Shot taken from a camera position on the side of the road filming a vehicle driving by.

RUNNING SHOT: Vehicle-to-vehicle filming from a camera mounted on a camera car, moving with the vehicle being filmed ("picture car").

SCRIMS: Diffusion material placed in front of lights to soften the effect.

SECOND UNIT: Filming done without the primary actors or director. Usually without sound. Can include inserts, stunts, or run-bys.

Shiny Boards: Reflectorized metal boards used to reduce the difference between light and shaded areas by bouncing sunlight into the darker areas.

SLATE: The numbered board held in front of the camera before a take; used to identify the film in the laboratory and cutting room.

SLOW MOTION: Film shot at a greater frames-per-second rate than the rate at which it will be projected, which slows down the motion.

SOUND CART: The wheeled cabinet on which sound recording equipment is placed to allow easy movement around the set.

SPECIAL EFFECTS: The name given to almost any unusual effect to create an illusion on film. Can be optical, mechanical, or pyrotechnic.

STRIKE: Remove set dressings, dismantle set, and remove equipment from a filming location.

STORY BOARD: A series of drawings used as visual representations of the shooting script. Sketches representing key situations and shots in the scripted scenes. Dialogue or indication of music, effects, etc. that appear below the pictures.

SWING GANG: A team of grips assigned to strike and clean up after filming. Although these grips are assigned to the art department, they are not the same people who prepared the area for filming.

SYNC: The intentional coinciding of an image with a given sound.

TAKE: A scene or part of a scene recorded on film and/or sound tape from each start to each stop of a camera and/or recorder. Each shot may be repeated in several takes, until a satisfactory result is achieved.

TOW SHOT: The vehicle being filmed is actually towed by a truck (often the camera car). This is generally required when filming dialogue between the driver and a passenger. Often the camera is mounted on the hood of the picture car, or on a door (side mount). Side mounts may widen the overall width of the vehicle to exceed the width of a single lane of traffic. Traffic control is usually needed to help the vehicle safely through traffic.

WET DOWN: Intentionally spraying water on a road or other surface to create a visual effect for filming or to minimize dust.

WILD TRACK: Sound recording such as sound effect or ambient noise not synchronized with film image.

XLS: Extreme Long Shot. Distant landscape or vast interior shot in which human figures appear relatively small.

ZOOM: The magnification of a certain area of the frame by bringing it optically to the full size of the screen and excluding the rest of the frame in the process.

THE AUTHOR'S
TOP TEN SOUTHWESTERN FILMS

One cannot view as many films as I have in preparing this book, and not begin to formulate a few lists. In compiling the following, I first had to establish a working definition of what constitutes a film classic. I finally settled on three criteria. First, any classic must provide—through dialogue and plot—the basic elements that actors can then use to create memorable characters (of course, it is not enough simply to have a fine script—only an actor, for example, with Henry Fonda's meticulous devotion to craft can successfully render a character as rich as Tom Joad in *The Grapes of Wrath)*. Second, the story must be timeless, and engage one of the great themes—love, death, war, evil, freedom—of human life. All enduring films speak to the eternal verities of the human condition. Third, the movie must be made according to the highest levels of technical craft (camera-work, musical score, editing) and, if possible, achieve some manner of stylistic innovation (break new ground cinematically). Much of this difficult narrative-building process is dependent upon the leadership skills and artistic abilities of the director—whether he or she reaches for excellence, or mediocrity, in the act of making a film (and inspires others in this regard).

The following list covers the sixty-year period from 1939 through 1999. In this era much about America and the world at large changed, primarily in terms of shifting political power, greater national wealth, and new technology. During that span of time, though, nothing about the devotion of national and international audiences to quality filmmaking altered. What made *Stagecoach* a success in 1939—strong characters, good story, superb film craft—also made *Butch Cassidy and the Sundance Kid* a success in 1969. The list represents every state in the Southwestern region (defined geographically in this book as having an arid landscape), except Colorado. The list does not include silent films. If it did it would include such classics as *Greed* or *The Iron Horse.* Nor does it include thematic Southwestern films, such as *A Fistful of Dollars*

or *The Treasure of the Sierrra Madre,* filmed outside the United States (Italy and Mexico, respectively). Southwestern films shot for the most part in a Hollywood studio (such as Humphrey Bogart and Bette Davis's *The Petrified Forest)* are also not represented here. Films that used the Southwestern region only marginally—such as *Rain Man* or *Forrest Gump*—are not included, although they are outstanding pictures. Nor are, regrettably, television movies (such as the brilliant *Lonesome Dove).* Finally, the list does not include all of the Southwestern films represented in the American Film Institute's 1998 list of the top one hundred American films, including Easy Rider and *High Noon.* It does, however, include some of the Southwestern films on that list: *Stagecoach, The Grapes of Wrath, The Searchers,* and *Butch Cassidy and the Sundance Kid.*

This, in summary, is a short list of cherished films that—in a variety of ways—attained about as much perfection as films are capable of. Several involved the performances of familiar actresses and actors, such as Marilyn Monroe and Clark Gable *(The Misfits)*, Claire Trevor and John Wayne *(Stagecoach)*. Others presented lesser-known ensembles (such as *The Milagro Beanfield War).* Quite a few performed well at the box office *(The Searchers)*. Others enjoyed more modest success *(Lonely Are the Brave)*. They are each superb narratives, the sort of film I would want with me on a deserted island, the sort of film I would put on a syllabus if I were to teach a semester-long class in Southwestern film.

Each reader will naturally have his or her own list. I would be interested in hearing from you in this regard—please feel free to send them to me at P.O. Box 102345, Denver, Colorado 80250.

1. Stagecoach (1939)

Stagecoach created the modern standard for the Western. Claire Trevor is perfect as Dallas, the prostitute looking to change her life, and John Wayne's performance as "The Ringo Kid" holds the entire picture together. What's more, the world was given its first good view of the magnificent spectacle of nature that is Monument Valley.

2. Tender Mercies (1983)

At the core of this film are two cinematic wonders—Horton Foote's screenplay and Robert Duvall's performance. Anyone who has ever lost his way on the journey (who hasn't?) and then been forced to find la vita nuova will be able to relate to the story of the country-western singer played by Duvall. The film captures the essence of the southwestern prairie—the hard light and eternal wind. It is filled with hope and optimism, even at its darkest moments.

3. Hud (1963)

Every performance in this complex film is exceptional—Paul Newman, Melvyn Douglas, Patricia Neal. All of the sadness and despair of the isolated rural life in Texas is poured into the movie, even more so than in McMurtry's earlier *The Last Picture Show.*

4. Lonely Are the Brave (1962)

This is the classic story about the changes that have so harshly transformed the American West over the last fifty years. Filmed in black and white, the picture is a stark portrait of the price of progress: the last cowboy, hopelessly in love with the wide open spaces and naturally wearing a white hat (Kirk Douglas), versus the self-serious city folk who must corral him and all he represents (Walter Matthau and others).

5. High Plains Drifter (1972)

This is the film that saw the maturation of Clint Eastwood as a major force in the Western. Much of what we would see in his later films—the understated acting presence, the unflinching portrait of official corruption, the ultimate triumph of the wronged individual—is present here. Mono Lake—a metaphor for all that is bleak and empty in the human spirit—proved to be the ideal setting for such a tale.

6. The Searchers (1956)

The Searchers is John Ford's most complex picture, as the chief character, Ethan Edwards (played by John Wayne), possesses as many deep flaws as admirable virtues. Although some might suggest that Wayne's best performance was as Captain Nathan Brittles in *She Wore a Yellow Ribbon,* his sympathetic depiction of Ethan Edwards required more skill. *The Searchers* captures all the visual splendor of Navajo Country.

7. The Grapes of Wrath (1940)

John Steinbeck's *The Grapes of Wrath* honestly explored the injustices and unpleasant truths at the core of the American experience. This film captures all of that, and more, with one of Henry Fonda's finest performances. Here we see nature's revenge—her literal wrath—on those who have abused her, as well as the indestructibility of the human spirit.

8. Butch Cassidy and the Sundance Kid (1969)

These two affable outlaws are doomed from the first moment, if only because what they seek—complete personal freedom—is unattainable. The wide-angle shots of the beautiful Painted Desert country in southern Utah are spectacular, as are the canyon scenes north of Durango, Colorado.

9. The Milagro Beanfield War (1988)

This comedic fable is set in some of the loveliest country in the Southwest—the Taos highlands. Here author John Nichols, and director Robert Redford, give the world a whimsical bit of magic realism, while at the same time lampooning all the destruction and chaos that unbridled human greed can inflict upon a landscape.

10. The Misfits (1961)

The conventional wisdom says that *The Misfits* is a flawed masterpiece, but life is flawed and all great works of art—from Shakespeare's *Hamlet* to Faulkner's *The Hamlet*—are flawed (as are, for that matter, all people). This film gave us the finest cinematic performances of both Clark Gable and Marilyn Monroe. What's more, the film actively involved the Western landscape as a character in the story—wild horses, big sky, empty desert.

Southwestern Films and the Academy Awards

(films made wholly or significantly in the Southwest)

1929 **In Old Arizona**
Best Actor (Warner Baxter)

1931 **Cimarron**
Best Screenplay (Howard Estabrook); Best Interior
Decoration (Max Ree)

1938 **The Cowboy and the Lady**
Best Sound Recording (Thomas Moulton)

1939 **Stagecoach**
Best Supporting Actor (Thomas Mitchell)

1940 **The Westerner**
Best Supporting Actor (Walter Brenann)

1940 **The Grapes of Wrath**
Best Actor (Henry Fonda)

1948 **The Treasure of the Sierra Madre**
[filmed in Mexico] Best Director (John Huston); Best
Supporting Actor (Walter Huston); Best Screenplay
(John Huston)

1948 **She Wore A Yellow Ribbon**
Best Cinematography

1952 **High Noon**
Best Actor (Gary Cooper); Best Scoring of a Dramatic Picture
(Dimitri Tiomkin); Best Song (Dimitri Tiomkin); Best Film
Editing (Elmo Williams, Harry Gerstad)

1952 **Viva Zapata!**
Best Supporting Actor (Anthony Quinn)

1954 **Broken Lance**
Best Screenplay (Philip Yordan)

1955 **Oklahoma!**
Best Scoring of a Musical Picture (Robert Russell Bennet,
Jay Blackton, Adolph Deutsch)

1956 **Giant**
Best Director (George Stevens)

1960 **The Alamo**
Best Cinematography

1960 **The Sandpiper**
Best Musical Score (Burt Bacharach)

1963 **Hud**
Best Actress (Patricia Neal); Best Supporting Actor
(Melvyn Douglas)

1963 **How the West Was Won**
Best Screenplay (James R. Webb); Best Cinematography
(James Wong Howe); Best Sound (MGM Sound
Department); Best film editing (Harold R. Kress)

1965 **Cat Ballou**
Best Actor (Lee Marvin)

1967 **Bonnie and Clyde**
Best Supporting Actress (Estelle Parsons)

1969 **True Grit**
Best Actor (John Wayne)

1969 **Butch Cassidy and the Sundance Kid**
Best Screenplay (William Goldman); Best Cinematography
(Conrad Hall); Best song (Burt Bacharach); Best Original
Score of a nonmusical picture (Burt Bacharach)

1971 **The Last Picture Show**
Best Supporting Actor (Ben Johnson); Best Supporting
Actress (Cloris Leachman)

1973 **The Great American Cowboy**
Best Documentary

1980 **Melvin and Howard**
Best Supporting Actress (Mary Steenburgen)

1983 **Terms of Endearment**
Best Picture, Best Actress (Shirley MacLaine), Best Supporting
Actor (Jack Nicholson), Best Director (James L. Brooks)

1983 **Tender Mercies**
Best Actor (Robert Duvall)

1988 **Rain Man**
Best Picture; Best Actor (Dustin Hoffman)

1995 **Forrest Gump**
Best Picture; Best Actor (Tom Hanks)

1995 **Leaving Las Vegas**
Best Actor (Nicholas Cage)

1997 **Casino**
Best Actress (Sharon Stone)

Western Shows on Network Television: A Selected List

Most of these programs were shot in the Los Angeles area, either on studio lots or on studio property in such locations as the Santa Monica Mountains (see description of the Santa Monica National Recreation Area in the California chapter).

The Adventures of Jim Bowie (starring Scott Forbes)—ABC: 1956–1958

The Adventures of Rin-Tin-Tin (starring Lee Aaker, James Brown, Joe Sawyer)—ABC/CBS: 1954–1964

Bat Masterson (starring Gene Barry)—NBC: 1957–1961

The Big Valley (starring Barbara Stanwyck, Linda Evans, Lee Majors)—ABC: 1965–1969

Bonanza (starring Lorne Greene, Dan Blocker, Michael Landon, Pernell Roberts)—NBC: 1959–1973

Branded (starring Chuck Connors and John Carradine)—NBC: 1965–1966

Broken Arrow (starring Michael Ansara and John Lupton)—ABC: 1956–1958

Cheyenne (starring Clint Walker)—ABC: 1957–1963

Dallas (starring Larry Hagman and Victoria Principal)—1979–1992

Death Valley Days (hosted by Ronald Reagan and Dale Robertson)—NBC: 1952–1972

Dick Powell's Zane Grey Theater (hosted by Dick Powell)—CBS: 1956–1962

F Troop (starring Forrest Tucker, Larry Storch, Melody Patterson)—ABC: 1965–1967

Gunsmoke (starring James Arness, Dennis Weaver, Ken Curtis)—CBS: 1955–1975

Have Gun—Will Travel (starring Richard Boone)—CBS: 1957–1963

Hopalong Cassidy (starring William Boyd)—NBC: 1948–1952

Iron Horse (starring Dale Robertson and Gary Collins)—ABC: 1966–1968

Maverick (starring James Garner)—ABC: 1957–1962

My Friend Flicka (starring Gene Evans)—ABC/CBS/NBC: 1957–1966

Rawhide (starring Clint Eastwood, Eric Fleming, Sheb Wooley)—CBS: 1958–1966

Tales of Wells Fargo (starring Dale Robertson)—NBC: 1957–1962

The Deputy (starring Henry Fonda)—NBC: 1959–1961

The Gabby Hayes Show (starring Gabby Hayes)—NBC: 1950–1951

The Gene Autry Show (starring Gene Autry)—ABC: 1950–1955

The Guns of Will Sonnet (starring Walter Brennan)—ABC: 1967–1969

The High Chaparral (starring Leif Erickson, Linda Cristal)—NBC: 1967–1971

The Life and Legend of Wyatt Earp (starring Hugh O'Brian)—ABC: 1955–1961

The Lone Ranger (starring Clayton Moore, Jay Silverheels, John Hart)—ABC/CBS: 1948–1961

THE RIFLEMAN (starring Chuck Connors)—ABC: 1958–1962

THE ROY ROGERS SHOW (starring Roy Rogers and Dale Evans)—NBC/CBS: 1951–1964

THE VIRGINIAN (starring James Drury and Douglas McClure)—NBC: 1962–1970

THE WILD WILD WEST (starring Robert Conrad)—CBS: 1965–1969

SKY KING (starring Robert Bray)—NBC: 1958–1961

WAGON TRAIN (starring Ward Bond)—NBC/ABC: 1957–1965

CITY AND STATE FILM COMMISSIONS

This list can be valuable to the reader in several ways. First, the city and state film commissions maintain detailed lists of all the films that were shot on location in their respective areas. These lists are available on request. Second, the city and state film commissions can often provide readers with fairly precise location information as to where and when films were shot. The commissions also maintain other archives, and can always be counted on to assist when questions arise.

Arizona

ARIZONA FILM COMMISSION—3800 North Central Avenue, Bldg. D, Phoenix, Arizona 85012 (602-280-1380; 800-523-6695; FAX 602-280-1384; E-Mail mopic@ep.state.az.us)

APACHE JUNCTION CHAMBER OF COMMERCE—P.O. Box 1747, Apache Junction, Arizona 85217-1747 (480-982-3141; 800-252-3141; FAX 480-982-3234)

COCHISE COUNTY FILM COMMISSION—1415 West Melody Lane, Building B, Bisbee, Arizona 85603 (520-432-9454; 520-432-5200; FAX 520-432-5016)

COTTONWOOD FILM COMMISSION—1010 South Main Street, Cottonwood, Arizona 86326 (520-634-7593; FAX 520-634-7594)

FLAGSTAFF FILM COMMISSION—1300 South Milton, Suite 125, Flagstaff, Arizona 86001 (520-779-7658; 800-595-7658; FAX 520-556-0940; E-Mail gfec@primenet.com)

GLOBE FILM COMMISSION—1360 North Broad Street, U.S. 60, P.O. Box 2539, Globe, Arizona, 85502 (520-425-4495; 800-804-5623; FAX 520-425-3410)

KINGMAN FILM COMMISSION—P.O. Box 1150, Kingman, Arizona 86402 (520-753-5100; FAX 520-753-1049)

PAGE-LAKE POWELL FILM COMMISSION—644 North Navajo Drive, P.O. Box 727, Page, Arizona 86040 (520-645-2741; FAX 520-645-3181; E-Mail chamber@page-lakepowell.com)

PHOENIX FILM COMMISSION—200 West Washington, 10th Floor, Phoenix, Arizona 85003-1611 (602-262-4850; FAX 602-534-2295)

PRESCOTT FILM COMMISSION—P.O. Box 2059, Prescott, Arizona 86302 (520-445-3500; FAX 520-776-6255)

SCOTTSDALE FILM OFFICE—7447 East Indian School Road, Suite 100, Scottsdale, Arizona 85251 (480-312-7828; FAX 480-312-7011)

SEDONA FILM COMMISSION—P.O. Box 2489, Sedona, Arizona 86339 (520-204-1123; FAX 520-204-1064)

TUCSON FILM OFFICE—P.O. Box 27210, Tucson, Arizona 85726-7210 (520-791-4000; 520-791-5093; FAX 520-791-5413)

WICKENBURG FILM COMMISSION—216 North Frontier Street, Wickenburg, Arizona 85390 (520-684-5479; FAX 520-684-5470; E-Mail wburgcoc@primenet.com)

YUMA FILM COMMISSION—850 West 32nd Street, Suite 6, Yuma, Arizona 85364 (520-341-1616; 520-726-4027; FAX 520-341-1685)

California

CALIFORNIA FILM COMMISSION—7080 Hollywood Boulevard, Suite 900; Hollywood, California 90028 (213-860-2960; 800-858-4PIX; FAX 213-860-2972; E-Mail FILMCA@aol.com)

ANTELOPE VALLEY FILM OFFICE—44933 North Fern Avenue, Lancaster, California 93534 (805-723-6090; FAX 805-723-5913; E-Mail jmcneil@city.lancaster.ca.us)

BIG BEAR LAKE FILM OFFICE—39707 Big Bear Boulevard, P.O. Box 10000, Big Bear Lake, California 92315 (909-878-3040; FAX 909-866-6766)

Tahoe Film Commission—542 Main Street, Placerville, California 95667 (916-626-4400; 800-457-6279; FAX 916-642-1624)

Imperial County Film Commission—940 West Main Street, Suite 208, El Centro, California 92242 (760-339-4290; 800-345-6437; FAX 760-352-7876)

Kern County Film Office—2101 Oak Street, PO. Box 1312, Bakersfield, California 93302 (805-861-2367; 800-500-KERN; FAX 805-861-2017)

Long Beach Film Office—333 West Ocean Boulevard, 13th Floor, Long Beach, California 90802 (310-570-5333; FAX 310-570-5335)

Los Angeles Entertainment Industry Development Office—7083 Hollywood Boulevard, 5th Floor, Hollywood, California 90028 (213-957-1000; FAX 213-463-0613; Internet www.eid.com)

Malibu City Film Commission—23555 Civic Center Way, Malibu, California 91360 (310-456-2489 x-236; FAX 310-456-5799; E-Mail kcollins@ci.malibu.ca.us)

Monterey County Film Commission—801 Lighthouse Avenue, P.O. Box 111, Monterey, California 93942-0111 (408-646-0910; FAX 408-655-9244; E-Mail mryfilm@aol.com)

Orange County Film Commission—2 Park Plaza, Suite 100, Irvine, California 92614 (714-476-2242; 800-628-8033; FAX 714-476-0513; E-Mail ocedc@orangecountyedc.com)

Palm Springs Desert Film Office—69-930 Highway 111, Suite 201, Rancho Mirage, California 92270 (619-770-9000; Fax 619-770-9001; Internet http://www.desert-resorts.com)

City of Pasadena Film Office—100 North Garfield Avenue, #103, Pasadena, California 91109 (818-405-4152; FAX 818-405-4785)

Riverside/San Bernardino Film Commission—301 East Vanderbilt Way, Suite 100, San Bernardino, California 92408 (909-890-1090; 800-500-4367; FAX 909-890-1088; E-Mail iefc@deltanet.com)

San Diego Film Commission—402 West Broadway, Suite 1000, San Diego, California 92101-3585 (619-234-3456; FAX 619-544-1351)

San Luis Obispo County Film Commission—1037 Mill Street, San Luis Obispo, California 93401 (805-541-8000; FAX 805-543-9498)

Santa Barbara County Film Commission—12 East Carrillo Street, Santa Barbara, California 93101 (805-966-9222; FAX 805-966-1728)

Santa Clarita Valley Film Bureau—23920 Valencia Boulevard, Suite 125, Santa Clarita, California 91355-2175 (800-4FILMSC; 805-259-4787; FAX 805-259-7304)

Santa Cruz County Film Commission—701 Front Street, Santa Cruz, California 95060; 408-425-1234; 800-833-3494; FAX 408-425-1260; E-Mail dopa@cruzio.com)

Vallejo/Solona County Film Commission—495 Mare Island Way, Vallejo, California 94590 (707-642-3653; 800-4-VALLEJO; FAX 707-644-2206; E-Mail vjocvb@visitvallejo.com)

Temecula Valley Film Council—P.O. Box 1786, Temecula, California 92593 (909-699-6267; FAX 909-694-1999)

City of West Hollywood Film Office—8300 Santa Monica Boulevard, West Hollywood, California 90069-4314 (213-848-6489; FAX 213-848-6561; E-Mail wehofilm@ci.west-hollywood.ca.us)

Colorado

Colorado Motion Picture & TV Commission—1625 Broadway, Suite #1700, Denver, Colorado 80202 (303-620-4500; FAX 303-620-4545; Internet http://www.coloradofilm.com)

Boulder County Film Commission—P.O. Box 73, Boulder, Colorado 80306 (303-442-1044; 800-444-0447; FAX 303-938-8837)

Colorado Springs Film Commission—104 South Cascade Avenue, Suite 104, Colorado Springs, Colorado 80903 (719-635-7506; 800-368-4748; FAX 719-635-4968; E-Mail film@coloradosprings-travel.com)

Denver Office of Art, Culture & Film—280 14th Street, Denver, Colorado 80202 (303-640-2686; FAX 303-640-2737)

Fort Collins/LKarimer County Film Office—420 South Howes Street, Suite 101, P.O. Box 1998, Fort Collins, Colorado 80522 (970-482-5821; FAX 970-493-8061;)

Fort Morgan Area Film Commission—710 East Railroad Avenue, P.O. Box 100, Fort Morgan, Colorado 80701 (970-867-4310; FAX 970-867-3039; E-Mail ssengle@twol.com)

Greeley/Weld County Film Commission—902 7th Avenue, Greeley, Colorado 80631 (970-352-3566; 800-449-3866; FAX 970-352-3572)

Yampa Valley Film Board—Box 772305, Steamboat Springs, Colorado 80477 (970-879-0882; FAX 970-879-2543; E-Mail info@steamboat-chamber.com)

Trinidad Film Commission—136 West Main Street, Trinidad, Colorado 81082 (719-846-9412; 800-748-1970; FAX 719-846-4550)

Nevada

Nevada Motion Picture Division—555 East Washington, Suite 5400, Las Vegas, Nevada 89101 (702-486-2711; FAX 702-486-2712; E-Mail danterh@aol.com)

Reno Area Motion Picture Office—5151 South Carson Street, Carson City, Nevada 89710 (800-336-1600; 702-687-4325; FAX 702-687-4450; E-Mail RHBIRD@aol.com)

New Mexico

New Mexico Film Office—1100 South St. Francis Drive, P.O. Box 20003, Santa Fe, New Mexico 87504-5003 (800-545-9871; 505-827-9810; FAX 505-827-9799; E-Mail linda@film.edd.state.nm.us)

Albuquerque TV & Film Office—20 First Plaza NW, Suite 601, P.O. Box 26866, Albuquerque, New Mexico 87126-6866 (505-842-9918; 800-733-9810; FAX 505-247-9101; E-Mail barnhill@abqcvb.org)

Las Cruces Film Commission—311 North Downtown Mall, Las Cruces, New Mexico 88001 (505-524-8521; 800-FIESTAS; FAX 505-524-8191)

Los Alamos County Film Commission—P.O. Box 460, Los Alamos, New Mexico 87544-0460 (505-662-8401; FAX 505-662-8399)

Texas

Texas Film Commission—P.O. Box 13246, Austin, Texas 78711 (512-463-9200; FAX 512-463-4114; E-Mail film@governor.texas.gov)

Amarillo Film Office—1000 South Polk Street, Amarillo, Texas 79101 (806-374-1497; 800-692-1338; FAX 806-373-3909; E-Mail amarcvb@arn.net)

Austin Film Office—201 East Second Street, Austin, Texas 78701 (512-404-4562; 800-926-2282; FAX 512-404-4564)

Dallas/Fort Worth Regional Film Commission—P.O. Box 610246, DFW Airport, Texas 75261-0246 (972-621-0400; 800-234-5699; FAX 972-929-0916; E-Mail 2filmdfwtexas@ntc-dfw.org)

El Paso Film Commission—#1 Civic Center, El Paso, Texas 79901 (915-534-0695; 800-351-6024; FAX 915-534-0686; E-Mail elpasotx@huntleigh.net)

Houston Film Commission—801 Congress, Houston, Texas 77002 (713-227-3100; 800-365-7575; FAX 713-223-3816)

Irving Texas Film Commission—6309 North O'Connor Road, Suite 222, Irving, Texas 75039-3500 (214-869-0303; 800-2-IRVING; FAX 214-869-4609)

San Antonio Film Commission—P.O. Box 2277, San Antonio, Texas 78230 (210-270-8700; 800-447-3327; FAX 210-270-8782; E-Mail Films@ci.Bat.tx.us)

Utah

Utah Film Commission—324 South State, Suite 500, Salt Lake City, Utah 84114-7330 (801-538-8740; 800-453-8824; FAX 801-538-8886; E-Mail cemain.lvondere@film.state.ut.us)

Central Utah Film Commission–100 East Center Street, Suite 3200, Provo, Utah 84606 (801-370-8390; 800-222-8824; FAX 801-370-8105; E-Mail ucadm.marilyn@state.ut.us)

Kanab/Kane County Film Commission–78 South 100 East, Kanab, Utah 84741 (435-644-5033; 800-SEE-KANE; FAX 435-644-5923; E-Mail kanetrav@xpresweb.com)

Moab to Monument Valley Film Commission–50 East Center #1, Moab, Utah 84532 (435-259-6388; 435-587-3235; FAX 435-259-6399; E-Mail mmvfc@uvol.com)

Park City Film Commission–P.O. Box 1630, Park City, Utah 84060 (801-649-6100; 800-453-1360; FAX 801-649-4132) Utah's Southwest Film Commission–906 North 1400 West, P.O. Box 1550, St. George, Utah 84771-1559 (435-628-4171; 800-233-8824; FAX 435-673-3540)

Southwestern National and State Parks, National Forests, and Bureau of Land Management Units Involved in Filming

Arizona

Apache/Sitgreaves National Forest–Forest Supervisor, 309 South Mountain Avenue, P.O. Box 640, Springerville, Arizona 85938 (520-333-4301)

Canyon de Chelly National Monument–P.O. Box 588, Chinle, Arizona 86503-0588 (520-674-5500)

Coconino National Forest–Forest Supervisor, 2323 East Greenlaw Lane, Flagstaff, Arizona 86004 (520-527-3600)

Coronado National Forest–Forest Supervisor, Federal Building, 300 West Congress Street, Tucson, Arizona 85701 (520-670-4552)

Glen Canyon National Recreation Area–P.O. Box 1507 Page, Arizona 86050-1507 (520-608-6404)

Monument Valley Tribal Park–Navajo Parks and Recreation Department, P.O. Box 308, Window Rock, Arizona 86515 (801-727-3353)

Organ Pipe Cactus National Monument–Route 1 Box 100, Ajo, Arizona 85321-9626 (520-387-6849)

Saguaro National Park–3693 South Old Spanish Trail, Tucson, Arizona 85730-5699 (520-733-5153)

California

Alabama Hills Recreation Area–Bureau of Land Management, Bishop Research Area 785 North Main Street, Suite E, Bishop, California 93514 (619-872-4881)

Algodones Dune Fields–Bureau of Land Management El Centro Resource Area, 1661 South 4th Street, El Centro, California 92243-4561 (619-337-4400)

Death Valley National Park–P.O. Box 579, Death Valley, California 92328-0579 (619-786-2331)

Inyo National Forest (Mono Lake)–U.S. Forest Service, P.O. Box 429, Lee Vining, California 93541 (619-647-3044)

Malibu Creek State Park–1925 Las Virgenes Road, Calabasas, California 91302 (818-880-0350)

Mojave National Preserve–P.O. Box 241, Barstow, California 92309 (619-733-4040)

Joshua Tree National Park–74485 National Park Drive, Twentynine Palms, California 92277-3597 (619-367-7511)

Santa Monica Mountains National Recreation Area–30401 Agouta Road, Suite 100, Agoura Hills, California 91301 (818-597-1036, ext 212; FAX 818-597-8357; E-Mail alice_allen@nps.gov)

Colorado

Colorado State Bureau of Land Management Office–2850 Youngfield Street, Lakewood Colorado 80215 (303-239-3600)

Grand Junction Bureau of Land Management Resource Area—764 Horizon Drive, Grand Junction, Colorado 81506 (303-243-6561)

Royal Gorge Bureau of Land Management Resource Area—3170 East Main Street, P.O. Box 2200, Canon City, Colorado 81215-2200 (719-275-0631)

Rio Grande National Forest—Forest Supervisor, 1803 West U.S. 160, Monte Vista, Colorado 81144 (719-852-5941)

San Juan National Forest—Forest Supervisor, 701 Camino Del Rio, Durango, Colorado 81301 (970-247-4874)

San Juan Bureau of Land Management Resource Area—701 Camino del Rio, Durango, Colorado 81301 (303-247-4082)

Nevada

Bureau of Land Management Office, State of Nevada—2881 Valley View Boulevard, Suite 16, Las Vegas, Nevada 89102 (702-873-8800)

Death Valley National Park (see California listing)

Humboldt National Forest—Forest Supervisor, 2035 Last Chance Road, Elko, Nevada 89801 (702-738-5171)

Lake Mead National Recreation Area—601 Nevada Highway, Boulder City, Nevada 89005 (702-293-8906)

New Mexico

Carlsbad Caverns National Park—3225 National Parks Highway, Carlsbad, New Mexico 88220-5381 (505-785-2232)

Carson National Forest—Forest Supervisor, P.O. Box 558, Taos, New Mexico 87571 (505-758-6200)

Santa Fe National Forest—Forest Supervisor, P.O. Box 1689, Santa Fe, New Mexico 87504 (505-988-6940)

White Sands National Monument—P.O. Box 1086, Holloman AFB, New Mexico 88330-1086 (505-479-6124)

Texas

Big Bend National Park—P.O. Box 129, Big Bend National Park, Texas 79834-0129 (915-477-2251)

Guadalupe Mountains National Park—HC 60 Box 400, Salt Flat, Texas 79847-9400 (915-828-3251)

Utah

Arches National Park—P.O. Box 907, Moab, Utah 84532-0907 (435-259-8161)

Bryce Canyon National Park—Bryce Canyon, Utah 84717-0001 (435-834-5322)

Canyonlands National Park—2282 South West Resource Boulevard, Moab, Utah 84532-8000 (435-259-7164)

Capitol Reef National Park—HC 70, Box 15, Torrey, Utah 84775-9602 (435-425-3791)

Glen Canyon National Park (see Arizona listing)

Goblin Valley State Park—885 East Main Street, Green River, Utah 84525 (435-564-3633; 800-322-3770)

Zion National Park—Zion National Park, Springdale, Utah 84767-1099 (435-772-3256)

The Best Filming Locations to Visit in the Southwest

What follows is a list, entirely subjective and in no particular order, of what the author has found to be the best (most beautiful, most interesting) film locations to visit in the American Southwest. Any one of these could easily be included in a family vacation. In several instances, a single trip can include several locations. For example, Moab is only a two-hour drive north on U.S. 191 from Monument Valley (accommodations can be found at Moab, Monticello, Blanding, Mexican Hat, or Kayenta). Similarly, anyone visiting Death Valley should motor on two hours west on State Routes 190/136 and visit the Alabama Hills and

Mount Whitney (staying at one of the finest and friendliest towns in the Southwest, Lone Pine). In Southern Arizona, a trip to the film set known as Old Tucson on the outskirts of Tucson could also take in the Algodones Dune Fields, the historic town of Tombstone, and the national monument at Fort Bowie on Apache Pass, where the battles between Apache chieftain Cochise and the U.S. cavalry really took place.

1. **Monument Valley (Arizona)**—Monument Valley is certainly the most representative landscape from the Golden Age of the Western film. The haunting scenery—mesas and buttes, wide-open desert, epic cloud formations—will stay with you forever. Visitors bring much-needed money into the cash-poor economy of the Navajo Reservation. Accommodations and/or camping can be found at Mexican Hat, Utah; at the end of the road in the Tribal Park (local Navajo families also have traditional eight-sided hogans that can be rented by the night); at Goulding's Lodge near the Park; and at Kayenta, Arizona.

2. **Page (Arizona)**—Glen Canyon National Recreation Area near Page is one of the most popular recreational areas in the Southwest. There is something here for everyone—houseboats, aerial tours, boat tours, horse-back riding, camping, fishing, hiking, rafting on the Colorado River below the dam—and all in a stunning desert landscape made famous by such films as *Broken Arrow* and *Maverick*. Page is a major regional city, with an airport and all the amenities.

3. **Alabama Hills (California)**—*Gunga Din. High Sierra. Joe Kidd.* The breathtaking landscapes of this unique BLM area at the base of Mount Whitney resonate with film history. Nearby Lone Pine has been serving the film industry and the tourist business for over seventy years—visitors will find it a friendly one-stoplight town offering all the customary services. Were it not for such a paucity of private land in the area, Lone Pine would be as developed as Palm Springs, Aspen, or Jackson Hole.

4. **Santa Monica National Recreation Area/Malibu Creek State Park (California)**—Anyone visiting Los Angeles should take the time to drive up the coastal highway to Malibu, turn right at Malibu Canyon Road, and explore these two extraordinary tracts of public land in the Santa Monica Mountains. Most visitors will recognize the scenery from such classic films as *Wells Fargo* and such beloved television shows as *M*A*S*H* and *Little House on the Prairie*. The old western town formerly used by Paramount is a great place to take the kids.

5. **Major Studios in Los Angeles (California)**—Those interested in the urban landscape, as represented in film, should definitely take the time to tour a studio while visiting Los Angeles. One of the best is Paramount Studios on Melrose Avenue in Hollywood (the main gate was featured in the 1950s television program Sunset Boulevard). Both Warner Brothers (Burbank) and Universal (Universal City) offer backlot tours as well.

6. **Santa Fe/Taos (New Mexico)**—Santa Fe and Taos are two of the oldest cities in the United States. Taos Pueblo may be the oldest continuously occupied community in North America (the core structure has been dated back eight hundred years). This area, with its unique Southwestern ambiance, has always had a special attraction for filmmakers, most recently for the acclaimed dramatic picture *Easy Rider* (Taos) and the popular comedy *Twins* (Santa Fe). Visitors will also find the third most important art market in the country (behind New York and San Francisco)—wonderful galleries abound in both towns.

7. **Old Tucson (Arizona)**—Old Tucson is the single finest film set that can be visited by the public in the Southwest. Located in the mountains just west of Tucson, Old Tucson is open year-round. Such film classics as *Arizona* and television series as *High Chaparral* were

filmed here. It's a good place to take the family and have pictures taken literally on the ground where John Wayne or, for that matter, Chevy Chase, Martin Short, and Steve Martin once stood *(Three Amigos!)*.

8. Moab (Utah)—No other area in the Southwest has provided the setting for more films than Moab. Three spectacular places stand out in Moab Country: Professor Valley, Arches National Park, and Canyonlands National Park—Island of the Sky District (the road to the plateau district passes through Sevenmile Canyon, an important filming location, and also leads to Thelma and Louise Point, seen in *Thelma and Louise,* and the Green River Overlook, seen in *The Greatest Story Ever Told).*

9. Death Valley (California)—Death Valley has been used extensively for filming since the silent era. It is the largest national park in the contiguous United States. Historically important filming locations include Zabriskie Point *(Greed),* the Sand Dunes near Stovepipe Wells *(Star Wars),* and Dante's Overlook *(Star Trek VI).* The best time to visit this unique area is from October through April—summers are somewhat hot. A full range of visitor services can be found—stores, restaurants, lodging, camping—at Furnace Creek adjacent to Park Headquarters.

10. White Sands (New Mexico)—The brilliant white gypsum sand dunes of White Sands National Monument have formed the backdrop for such classic Southwestern films as *Hang 'Em High* and *Lonesome Dove.* This is an exotically beautiful area that has to be seen to be believed—a miniature version of the Saharan Desert just a few hours north of El Paso. Most visitors to the monument stay in nearby Alamagordo.

Selected Films of the Southwestern Region and their Fictional Sources

Apache Territory	Louis L'Amour, *The Last Stand at Papago Wells*
Blood on the Moon	Luke Short, *Gunman's Choice*
Broken Arrow	Elliot Arnold, *Blood Brothers*
By the Light of the Western Stars	Zane Grey, *By the Light of the Western Stars*
Cat Ballou	Roy Chanslor, *The Ballad of Cat Ballou*
Cheyenne Autumn	Willa Cather, *Cheyenne Autumn*
Death of a Gunfighter	Lewis Patten, *Death of a Gunfighter*
East of Eden	John Steinbeck, *East of Eden*
Fire on the Mountain	Edward Abbey, *Fire on the Mountain*
Fort Apache	James Bellah, "Massacre" (short story)
Gunsmoke	Norman Fox, *Roughshod*
Hombre	Elmore Leonard, *Hombre*
Hondo	Louis L'Amour, *Hondo*
Hud	Larry McMurtry, *Horseman, Pass By*
Jeremiah Johnson	Vardis Fisher, *Mountain Man*
Lonely Are the Brave	Edward Abbey, *The Brave Cowboy*
Lonesome Dove	Larry McMurtry, *Lonesome Dove*
McCabe and Mrs. Miller	Edmund Naughton, *McCabe*
My Darling Clementine	Stuart Lake, *Wyatt Earp, Frontier Marshal*
Old Yeller	Fred Gipson, *Old Yeller*
Red River	B. Chase, *The Blazing Guns on the Chisolm Trail*
Rio Conchos	Clair Huffaker, *Guns of Rio Conchos*
Rio Grande	James Bellah, "Mission with No Record" (short story)

SHE WORE A YELLOW RIBBON	James Bellah, "War Party" (short story)	THE OX-BOW INCIDENT	Walter Van Tilburg Clark, *The Ox-Bow Incident*
STAGECOACH	Ernest Haycox, "Stage to Lordsburg" (short story)	THE PROFESSIONALS	Frank O'Rourke, *A Mule for the Marquesa*
TERMS OF ENDEARMENT	Larry McMurtry, *Terms of Endearment*	THE SEARCHERS	Alan Le May, *The Searchers*
THE COMANCHEROS	Paul Wellman, *The Comanchero*	THE SPOILERS	Rex Beach, *The Spoilers*
THE COWBOYS	William Dale Jennings, *The Cowboys*	THE TRACK OF THE CAT	Walter Van Tilburg Clark, *The Track of the Cat*
THE DARK COMMAND	W. R. Burnett, *The Dark Command*	THE TREASURE OF THE SIERRA MADRE	B. Traven, *The Treasure of the Sierra Madre*
THE GRAPES OF WRATH	John Steinbeck, *The Grapes of Wrath*		
THE LAST PICTURE SHOW	Larry McMurtry, *The Last Picture Show*	THE UNFORGIVEN (1940 version)	Alan LeMay, *The Unforgiven*
THE MARK OF ZORRO	Johnson McCully, *The Curse of Capostrano*	THE VIRGINIAN	Owen Wister, *The Virginian*
THE MILAGRO BEANFIELD WAR	John Nichols, *The Milagro Beanfield War*	TRUE GRIT	Charles Portis, *True Grit*

FURTHER READING

There are thousands of books and articles on film. What follows are a few texts that have been helpful to me along the way. The list is meant to be selective and not comprehensive. Although many fine titles are out of print, most books can be ordered through the Inter-Library Loan Department of your local public library.

Agel, Henri, ed., *Le Western*. Paris: Lettres Modernes, 1961.

Bazin, Andre. *What is Cinema?* Vol. ii. Trans. Hugh Gray. Berkley: University of California Press, 1971.

Bellour, Raymond and Patrick Brion eds., *Le Western*. Rev. ed. Paris: Union Generale d'Editions, 1969.

Bingham, Dennis. *Acting Male: Masculinities in the Films of James Stewart, Jack Nicholson and Clint Eastwood*. New Brunswick, NJ: Rutgers University Press, 1994.

Bold, Christine. *Selling the Wild West: Popular Western Fiction, 1860–1960*. Bloomington: Indiana University Press, 1987.

Buscombe, Edward, ed., *Stagecoach*. London: British Film Institute, 1992.

———. *The BFI Companion to the Western*. New York: Atheneum, 1988.

Byron, Stuart. "*The Searchers:* Cult Movie of the New Hollywood," *New York Magazine* March 5, 1979.

Caelti, John G. *The Six-Gun Mystique*. Bowling Green: Bowling Green University Press, 1971.

Cook, David A. *A History of Narrative Film*. New York: Norton, 1981.

Didion, Joan. "John Wayne: A Love Song." In *Slouching Towards Bethlehem*. New York: Farrar, Straus & Giroux, 1982.

Doane, Mary Ann. *The Desire to Desire: The Woman's Film of the 1940s*. Bloomington: Indiana University Press, 1987.

Frantz, Joe B. and Julian Ernest Choate. *The American Cowboy: The Myth and the Reality*. London: Thames and Hudson, 1956.

Frayling, Chrostopher. *Spaghetti Westerns: Cowboys and Europeans from Karl May to Sergio Leone*. London: Routledge and Kegan Paul, 1981.

French, Philip. *Westerns*. Rev. ed. London: Secker & Warburg, 1973.

Gallagher, Tag. *John Ford: The Man and His Films*. Berkeley: University of California Press, 1986.

Garfield, Brian. *Western Films*. New York: Rawson, 1982.

Graham, Don and William T. Pilkington. *Western Movies*. Albuquerque: University of New Mexico Press, 1979.

Grant, Barry Keith. *Film Genre Reader*. Austin: University of Texas Press, 1986.

Henderson, Brian. "*The Searchers*: An American Dilemma." *Film Quarterly* 34 (Winter 1980-81): 9-23.

Hyams, Jay. *The Life and Times of the Western Movie*. New York: W. H. Smith, 1983.

Jeffords, Susan. *Hard Bodies: Hollywood Masculinity in the Reagan Era*. New Brunswick, NJ: Rutgers University Press, 1994.

Kirkley, Donald H. *A Descriptive Study of the Network Television Western During the Seasons 1955–1963*. New York: Arno Press, 1979.

Kitses, Jim. *Horizons West–Anthony West, Budd Boetticher, Sam Peckinpah: Studies of Authorship with the Western*. London: Thames & Hudson, 1969.

Lahue, Kalton C. *Winners of the West: The Sagebrush Heroes of the Silent Screen*. New York: Barnes and Company, 1970.

Lenihan, John H. *Showdown: Confronting Modern America in the Western Film*. Chicago: University of Chicago Press, 1980.

McClure, Arthur and Ken D. Jones. *Heroes, Heavies and Sagebrush*. New York: Barnes and Company, 1972.

McGhee, Richard D. *John Wayne: Actor, Artist, Hero*. Jefferson, NC: McFarland & Co., 1990.

Mitchell, Lee Clark. *Westerns: Making the Man in Fiction and Film*. Chicago: University of Chicago Press, 1996.

Nachbar, Jack. *Western Films: An Annotated Critical Bibliography*. New York: Garland, 1982.

Parks, Rita. *The Western Hero in Film and Television: Mass Media Mythology*. Ann Arbor, MI: UMI Research Press, 1982.

Parish, James Robert and Michael R. Pitts. *The Great Western Pictures*. Metuchen, NJ: Scarecrow Press, 1976.

Place, J. A. *The Western Films of John Ford*. Seacaucus: Citadel Press, 1974.

Scott, Kenneth W. *Zane Grey, Born to the West: A Reference Guide*. Boston: G. K. Hall, 1979.

Seydor, Paul. *Peckinpah: The Western Films*. Urbana: University of Illinois Press, 1980.

Sklar, Robert. *Movie-Made America: A Social History of American Movies*. New York: Random House, 1975.

Slotkin, Richard. *Gunfighter Nation: the Myth of the Frontier in Twentieth-Century America*. New York: Atheneum, 1992.

Stanton, Bette. *Where God Put the West: Movie Making in the Desert from Moab to Monument Valley*. Moab, UT: Moab to Monument Valley Film Commission, 1994.

Steckmesser, Kent Ladd. *The Western Hero in History and Legend*. Norman: University of Oklahoma Press, 1965.

Tuska, Jon. *The Filming of the West*. New York: Doubleday, 1976.

Wright, Will. *Six Guns and Society: A Structural Study of the Western*. Berkeley: University of California Press, 1975.

INDEX

NOTE: *Italic page numbers indicate photographs, film stills, and posters. Titles of movies are followed by dates; books, plays, and television titles are indicated as such within parentheses and are without dates.*

ABOUT THE AUTHOR

Born in Cincinnati, Ohio, JOHN A. MURRAY holds degrees in English from the University of Colorado and the University of Denver. He is a former professor of English at the University of Alaska, Fairbanks, where he also directed the graduate degree program in professional writing. Murray is the author of over thirty works of nonfiction, including *Desert Awakenings: A Unique Journey Through America's Southwest* (NorthWord Press, 1998), *Cactus Country: The Deserts of the American Southwest* (Roberts Rinehart, 1996), and *The Colorado Plateau: A Complete Guide to the National Parks and Monuments of Southern Utah, Northern Arizona, Western Colorado, and Northwestern New Mexico* (Northland, 1998).